First World War
and Army of Occupation
War Diary
France, Belgium and Germany

25 DIVISION
7 Infantry Brigade
Devonshire Regiment
9th (Service) Battalion
1 September 1918 - 29 June 1919

WO95/2244/3

The Naval & Military Press Ltd
www.nmarchive.com
Published in association with The National Archives

Published by

The Naval & Military Press Ltd

Unit 10 Ridgewood Industrial Park,

Uckfield, East Sussex,

TN22 5QE England

Tel: +44 (0) 1825 749494

www.naval-military-press.com

www.nmarchive.com

This diary has been reprinted in facsimile from the original. Any imperfections are inevitably reproduced and the quality may fall short of modern type and cartographic standards.

© **Crown Copyright**
Images reproduced by permission of The National Archives, London, England, 2015.

Contents

Document type	Place/Title	Date From	Date To
Heading	WO95/2244-3		
Heading	9th Bn Devon Regt Sep 1918-Jun 1919 From Italy 7 Div. 20 Bde		
War Diary	Montrecehio Maggcove Italy	01/09/1918	15/09/1918
War Diary	France	16/09/1918	16/09/1918
War Diary	Canchy	17/09/1918	27/09/1918
War Diary	Franvillers	28/09/1918	30/09/1918
Miscellaneous	A Form Messages And Signals.	17/09/1917	17/09/1917
War Diary	Montauban-Villa Faucon	01/10/1918	01/10/1918
War Diary	Villa Faucon Ronssoy	02/10/1918	02/10/1918
War Diary	Ronssoy Quenemont Farm-Line	03/10/1918	11/10/1918
War Diary	Elincourt	12/10/1918	17/10/1918
War Diary	Elincourt Maurois	18/10/1918	18/10/1918
War Diary	Maurois Fassiaux Line	19/10/1918	30/10/1918
War Diary	Pommereuil-Le Cateau	31/10/1918	31/10/1918
Miscellaneous	Narrative Of Operations That Took Place On October 3rd To 11th 1918		
Miscellaneous	Account Of Operations 10/30th Oct 1918	31/10/1918	31/10/1918
War Diary	Le Cateau	01/11/1918	03/11/1918
War Diary	Pommereuil	04/11/1918	08/11/1918
War Diary	Landrecies	09/11/1918	13/11/1918
War Diary	Pommereuil	14/11/1918	29/11/1918
War Diary	Quievy	30/11/1918	30/11/1918
Miscellaneous	9th (Ser) Battalion The Devonshire Regiment.		
Miscellaneous			
Miscellaneous	W.24.6 1520		
Miscellaneous	9th Drum Regt	16/11/1918	16/11/1918
Miscellaneous	Instructions To Advance on 6/11/18 Ref. Map 57a 1/40.000	06/11/1918	06/11/1918
War Diary	Quievy	01/12/1918	31/12/1918
War Diary	Quievy	01/01/1919	03/01/1919
War Diary	Englefontaine	03/01/1919	31/01/1919
Miscellaneous	7th Infantry Brigade Transport Competition		
Miscellaneous	7th Infantry Brigade Transport Competition.	22/01/1919	22/01/1919
War Diary	Englefontaine	01/02/1919	19/02/1919
War Diary	Solesmes	20/02/1919	20/02/1919
War Diary	Cambrai	21/02/1919	28/02/1919
War Diary	Cambrai	01/03/1919	27/03/1919
Heading	9th (S) Battalion The Devonshire Regt War Diary For Month Ending 30th April 1919		
War Diary	Cambrai	12/04/1919	30/04/1919
Heading	9th (S) Battalion The Devonshire Regt War Diary For May 1919		
War Diary	Cambrai	01/05/1919	25/05/1919
War Diary	Cambrai France	01/06/1919	19/06/1919
War Diary	Cambrai	24/06/1919	29/06/1919

No 5/2244/3

25TH DIVISION
7TH INFY BDE

9TH BN DEVON REGT
SEP 1918-JUN 1919

FROM ITALY. 7 DIV. 20 Bde

Army Form C. 2118.

WAR DIARY
or
INTELLIGENCE SUMMARY.
(Erase heading not required.)

9 Devon

Sep 18 to June 19

36D

Place	Date	Hour	Summary of Events and Information	Remarks and references to Appendices
MAGGIORE ITALY	1/9/18		Divine Service. Capt H.G. Wilson rejoined from hospital.	
	2/9/18		Coy training on assault course. Musketry by Coys. Reserve Lewis gunners firing on Range. Devils at race attached to Battalion.	
	3/9/18		Divisional Sports at TRISSINO	
	4/9/18		Coys training on Range. Gunnery & application. Individual training.	
	5/9/18		Battalion scheme. Night Operations. 800 Parade.	
	6/9/18		Coy training on Hill climbing, Day Outpost Schemes, Gunnery, By Price, Lewis Gun, Signalling & scouting instruction. Night Operation. 1805 Compass Marching. Lte J.G. Benjamin rejoined from leave. Lte A. Wormell rejoined from leave. No 2. Coy PT Team went 3rd in Army Area PT met. 209 points	
	7/9/18		Training on Range. Assault Course.	
	8/9/18		Divine Service. Bde Church Parade.	
	9/9/18		Coy training on Hand Grids, Musketry & Firing on Range. Lewis Gunners firing on Range, Individual training, Sorting Coys. teams. Battalion Concert very successful.	
	10/9/18		Battalion scheme. Picket withdrawal after covering a retiring force into new attacked enemy position, Lewis Gun Instruction 6-12.30.	
	11/9/18		Training in Bns. Climbing & Rifle 40 Regiment for attack, Lewis Gunners, trials for Battalion Bucks attached to Battalion.	
	12/9/18		Battn Parade at 70 the Training Area. Lecture arranged by Div Commanders. Blenders wood engine, Rhode Street lecture in a AD issued Hostility of Artillery. It at Hordeng a genuer from 20th Tr Battery. Hte Edward Gregson from Leave.	

September 1918

Army Form C. 2118.

WAR DIARY
or
INTELLIGENCE SUMMARY.
(Erase heading not required.)

Instructions regarding War Diaries and Intelligence Summaries are contained in F.S. Regs., Part II. and the Staff Manual respectively. Title pages will be prepared in manuscript.

Place	Date	Hour	Summary of Events and Information	Remarks and references to Appendices
MONTECCHIO MAGGIORE	13/9/18		Entrained at Tavernelle in two trains for France on the Orders attached.	
	14/9/18 15/9/18		En Route for France.	
	16/9/18		Detrained at La RIVIER and marched to billets at Jancy, 1LAG 73/14 informed from SIRMIONE	
	17/9/18		Coy Inspection. Lewis gun Equipment Box Exhausive	
	18/9/18		Coy Training. Specialist offrs & Senrs & NCOs & NCO Lewis gunners from Prery.	
			Coy Training. Specialist training.	
	19/9/18		Training. An attack by four Gen Instruction Lectures by the Go Officers sent Pierced informers at STRIGUEN.	
	20/9/18		In billets in CANCHY, by raising these Relayout attackly, twenty of Drovegos, Lewis gun Selec from 9am - 12.30am.	
	21/9/18		In billets in CANCHY, Divine service. The following FAREWELL ORDER was received from 20th Infantry Bde.	
			The Brigadier cannot allow the 9th Bn Devonshire Regt whom he has had the honour to have under his Command for the last two years to leave the Brigade without expressing on his behalf and on behalf of the Brigade, their deep sorrow at parting with these old comrades.	
			The 9th Bn Devonshire Regt have always shown the highest standard of discipline and efficiency. They have always done bravest.	
			T.T.O

D.D. & I., London, E.C.
(A10250) W.W5300/P7113 750,000 2/15 Sch. 82 Forms/C2118/16

September 1918

WAR DIARY
or
INTELLIGENCE SUMMARY.
(Erase heading not required.)

Army Form C. 2118.

Place	Date	Hour	Summary of Events and Information	Remarks and references to Appendices
CANCHY	22/9/18		They have to select a site as near possible to do it. They have the Brigade with the highest refutation and the Brigadier wishes them the best of luck whenever they go.	
"	23/9/18		Battalion Scheme, Post Functional colours being worn on S.D. jackets.	
"	24/9/18		Buses allotted to Battalion	
"	29/9/18		In Billets in CANCHY, Colours Order Dress, Bombing, Colour sewing on Divisional sign.	
"	30/9/18		Firing on Range. Patches sewing on Divisional Colours.	
"	27/9/18		Training in gunnery, bombs to cent entrained at ST RIQUIER.	
"	28/9/18		Battalion detrained at ALBERT and marched to FRANVILLERS.	
Franvillers	29/9/18		Battalion entrained at FRANVILLERS for HARDICOURT	
	30/9/18		Battalion in shelters at HARDICOURT. Specialist training, Rifle Grenade, Officers Other Ranks 75 H. 34	

Strength of Battalion 30/9/18

Sept 30th 1918.

M.W. Beaucourt Major
for Lt. Col.
Comdg 9th (S) Bn The Devonshire Regt.

"A" Form
MESSAGES AND SIGNALS.

Army Form C. 2121
(In pads of 100.)

No. of Message............

Prefix......... Code.........m.	Words	Charge	This message is on a/c of :	Recd. at......m.
Office of Origin and Service Instructions	Sent		..................Service.	Date.............
....	At ....m.			From ....
....	To			
....	By		(Signature of "Franking Officer")	By..............

TO	25th Division G		

Sender's Number.	Day of Month.	In reply to Number.	AAA
S146/87/3	17th		

Herewith War Diary for October of the 9th Bn Devonshire Regt aaa Please acknowledge receipt

From 9th Inf Bde

W Pickley Capt
for Brig Gen

WAR DIARY
or
INTELLIGENCE SUMMARY.

(Erase heading not required.)

Army Form C. 2118.

October 1918.

9 Devons

Vol 37

37D

Place	Date	Hour	Summary of Events and Information	Remarks and references to Appendices
MONTAUBAN	1/10/18		Bn. left MONTAUBAN Area and marched to VILLA FAUCON. Billetted in shelters.	
VILLA FAUCON	2/10/18		Bn. had a attack in the morning. Left VILLA FAUCON at 16.00 hrs and marched to camp at RONSSOY.	
RONSSOY – QUENEMONT FARM LINE	3/10/18		Bn. standing to until 14.30 hrs when it moved to QUENEMONT FARM where Brigade concentrated. See Narrative of Operations 3rd/11th Bn. (attached)	
	4/10/18		See Narrative of Operations 3rd/11th Bn.	
See Narrative of Operations	5/10/18		Ditto. Capt. R.P.PRIDHAM. M.C. rejoined Bn. Details from Senior Officers Course Aldershot.	
	6/10/18		Ditto.	
	7/10/18		Ditto.	
	8/10/18		Ditto.	
	9/10/18		Ditto. 2/Lt L. ELWOOD joined Bn. Details.	
	10/10/18		Ditto.	
	11/10/18		Bn. was relieved after dark and marched back to billets at FINSURT.	
ELINCOURT	12/10/18		Bn. reorganizing and cleaning up billets. The following officers joined Bn.:— Lieuts R.P. YEATMAN, W.J. HYATT, 2/Lts S.A.J. GRIFFIN, R. COX, J. TC. HOLLOWAY, W. VERRIN, J.H. BLACKLER, W.W. HIGGS.	
	13/10/18		Church Parade.	
	14/10/18		Specialist Training and cleaning up vicinity of billets. Div. Gas Officer inspected Box Respirators. 2/Lt E.T.B. SHEPHERD joined Bn.	
	15/10/18		Specialist Training and cleaning up of village.	
	16/10/18		Specialist Training and cleaning of village. Bn. reorganized on two-Coy basis. Capt SCHUH. M.C. assumed command of No 1 Coy. Capt PRYNNE of No 2 Coy. Capt PRIDHAM. M.C. assumed duties of 2 i/c vice Major BRUNICARDI. M.C. to hospital 14/10/18.	

Army Form C. 2118.

WAR DIARY
or
INTELLIGENCE SUMMARY.
(Erase heading not required.)

October 1918

Instructions regarding War Diaries and Intelligence Summaries are contained in F. S. Regs., Part II. and the Staff Manual respectively. Title pages will be prepared in manuscript.

Place	Date	Hour	Summary of Events and Information	Remarks and references to Appendices
ELINCOURT	17/10/18		Specialist Training and cleaning up of village. Bn. at one hours notice from 12.00 hrs.	
	18/10/18		Bn. Left ELINCOURT at 11.00 hrs and marched to billets at MAUROIS	
MAUROIS	19/10/18		Bn. left MAUROIS at 04.50 hrs and marched to TASSIAUX Wood. Brigade concentrated Left of TASSIAUX at 16.45 hrs and took up Mastline to Bde Reserve. Bn left at 12.30 G.S. joined Bn. Details. Capt. R.P. PRIDHAM MC assumed command of Bn.	
MAUROIS LINE TASSANY LINE			See Narrative of Operations 19th/30th Octr.	
	20/10/18		Ditto	
	21/10/18		Ditto	
	22/10/18		Ditto	
	23/10/18		Ditto	
	24/10/18		Ditto	
	25/10/18		Ditto	
	26/10/18		2/Lt W. PEARCE and C.S.R. FARMER joined Bn. Details	
	27/10/18		A/Col H.I. STOREY D.S.O. assumed command of Bn. vice Capt. R.P. PRIDHAM MC	
	28/10/18		2/Lt. H.H.T. TAYLOR and J.T. DOBBS joined Bn. Details	
	29/10/18		2/Lt. I.D. BISHOP joined Bn. Details	
	30/10/18		2/Lt. A. PERICLOOD and R.J. TURNER joined Bn. Details. Bn. was relieved and marched back to billets at PONMEREUIL. 2/Lt. E.U. MURRAY joined Bn.	
PONMEREUIL LE CATEAU	31/10/18		Bn. left PONMEREUIL at 11.00 hrs and marched to billets at LE CATEAU. Strength of Bn. 21/10/18 — 37 Officers. 571 O.R.	

See Narrative of Operations.

NARRATIVE OF OPERATIONS THAT TOOK PLACE ON OCTOBER 3rd - 11th 1918

3rd On the afternoon of the 3rd of October the Battalion which was camped at RONSSOY received orders at 1500 hrs to move at once to QUENNEMONT FARM. Here Battalion and Coy Commanders were ordered to go forward and make arrangements for a relief which was to take place that night.
The Battalion was to relieve the 26th and 28th Australian Infantry Battalions in the BEUREVOIR Sector.
      Nos 1 and 2 Coys to be in the Front Line
      No. 3 Coy Support No. 4 Coy Reserve
      Battn H.Qrs with Reserve Coy.

4th The Battalion commenced the relief at 0330 hrs.
During the relief at 0515 an Officer of the 100th M.G.Battn delivered a dispatch from Bde ordering the Battalion to attack at 0610 hr
On receipt of these orders, as it was impossible to get the Coy Commanders together in time, written orders were issued to the Companies as follows.
No.1 Coy on the right was to attack BELLE VUE FARM
No.3 Coy in the centre to attack trenches at B" central
No.2 Coy on left to attack GUZENCOURT FARM
The orders were issued at 0630.
The runners delivering the messages found great difficulty in finding O.C. Coys as relief was still in progress.
The Coys detailed for the attack advanced at 0830
No.4 Coy was kept in Reserve as I did not consider it practicable to carry out the Bde order namely that this Coy was to mop up BEAUREVOIR from the North.
At 0930 message was sent off from the left Coy(No.2 Coy) and received at 1035 that they were held up by M.G. fire from both flanks.
At 0940 2/Lt C.Sutton M.C. was sent out by me to find out the situation. He returned to Battn H.Qrs at 1130 and reported that the left Coy had had to fall back on to its original line.
Centre Coy had also withdrawn to Front Line as it had come under heavy fire from BELLE VUE FARM and GOZENCOURT FARM.
No. 1 Coy on the right had taken BELLE VUE FARM and proceeding high ground beyond but coming under heavy M.G. Fire from BEAUREVOIR and being counter attacked as well, it was forced to withdraw to original position.
Touch had not yet been gained with Battn on Right.
Report was sent to Bde at 1200 giving above information also reporting that neither flank was in touch with Units on flanks.
At 1415 message was received from Bde sent off at 1106 that ZUNO was holding Trench system North of PROSPECT HILL on one left.
O.C. No.2 Coy sent out a patrol at dusk and obtained touch.
Orders were then received that the 75th Infty Bde were attacking at 0600 the morning of the 5th 9th Devons would remain in the line until the attacking Battns had passed through. Then the Battn would concentrate at B 15 d central. The operation was carried out successfully.

5th No. 4 Coy (Reserve Coy) and Battn H.Qrs arrived there at about 0830 when it was found that a Coy of 20th and 21st Manchester Regt were held up by M.G. fire from BEAUREVOIR. No.4 Coy proceeded to reinforce them.
After the advance had continued the Battn was withdrawn to the Quarry B15c3.1 and vicinity of TORRENS CANAL where it remained for that day and night and the following day.

6th On the night of the 6/7th the Battalion relieved elements of the
                                                continued

contd.

20th and 21st Manchesters in the Front Line from the Cemetery inclusive to the Track over TORRENS CANAL. Two Companies in the Front Line, One in Support about B 16 d central, One Coy in Reserve B 16 a
The 21st Manchesters sent out a patrol to PONCHAUX at 2330
9th Devons sent out a Patrol under an Officer at 2330 to investigate practice trenches B 11 c central and ascertain what damage had been done by bombardment which had taken place that afternoon.
The Patrol got within 50 yards of the objective and then they came under heavy M.G. fire, they heard work being carried on in the trenches and it was apparently held strongly.

7th There was a conference held on the 7th at Bde H.Qrs details for the attack on the 8th were discussed.

8th On the night of the 7/8th the Battn took over the frontage allotted to it, namely the LE CATEAU ROAD on the Right to B 17 a 3 6 (eastern corner of Cemetery) on left. One Platoon of the right Coy was on Eastern side of LE CATEAU ROAD overlapping with an American Battn One section from the left Coy overlapped with the South Africans on our left.
The Battn was formed up with Nos 1 and 4 Coys in FRONT LINE Nos 2 and 3 Coys in Support 300 yards in rear. All Coys reported that they were in position by 0430.
At Zero minus 3 mins the leading Coys crept forward close under the barrage and as soon as barrage lifted advanced to the attack, prior to this hostile shelling and M.G. fire had been somewhat heavy, the the enemy was using tracer bullets from his M.G's in addition hostile Aeroplanes dropped bombs on our troops just prior to the assualt.
About 0530 wounded and prisoners began to appear, wounded reported the village of PONCHAUX and that we were advancing beyond the village
At 0600 runner reported from No. 3 Coy that village had been taken and mopped up. Prisoners in large numbers now appeared. Battn H.Qrs then moved forward to catch up the advance, which they did at the Spur W of BRONX Farm.
At 0700 following message was sent to Bde.
"D.N. 31 Front line 500 yds S.W. of SONIA WOOD AAA Everything going well AAA Bn H.Qrs on Spur 200 yds N.W. BRONX FARM AAA"
Advance continued with only slight opposition from M.G's which were successfully dealt with by Tanks.
At 0820 the following message was sent to Bde.
"Am consolidating trench system running through SONIA WOOD AAA Am in touch on both flanks AAA Just been reported by a Sergt 20th that they are held up on right AAA They are about 700 yds S.E. of the LE CATEAU ROAD and there are no Americans on their right"
At 0930 PUTU reported they were meeting with no opposition.
The Battn that evening moved and took up a position along the line of the Railway U27 b 4 0 U 27 b central U 21 c 0 0
Orders were received that the Battn was to be prepared to continue the advance at 0530 next morning the 9th inst. At 0545 the Divisional Commander personally ordered the Battn to advance to a position near Western Edge of BUITRY WOOD. The Battn remained there that day and bivouaced in the wood the night 9/10th.

10th The advance was continued next morning at 0530 the Battn together with 20th Manchesters supporting 75th Inf Bde.

10th & 11th The Battn remained in Support to the 75th Inf Bde till withdrawn on the evening of the 11th inst.

Lieut Colonel
Comdg 9th (S) Battn The Devonshire Regiment.

Casualties for the period 3rd to 11th inclusive were:-

	Officers	Other Ranks
Killed	3	54
Wounded	9	158
Missing		1

2/Lt. S.P. Tozer 8/10/18
2/Lt. A.S. Bridgewater "
Lt. Haswell "

Account of Operations 19/30th Oct 1918
==

9th (S) Battn The Devonshire Regiment

19th   On the night of the 18/19th the Battalion took up a position in Brigade Reserve along the Sunken Road in Q II.b and Q II. C

~~20th~~   In Brigade Reserve Q 11.b and Q;11;c;

20th   -- ~~ditto~~ --
Draft of 124 O.R. joined the Battalion night of 20/21st
On the night of 20th/21st owing to the Brigade extending to the left, one Coy was placed at the disposal of O.C. 20th Manchester Regt for use in case of a counter-attack. No 1 Coy which was close to 20th Manchester Hqrs was detailed for this purpose.

21st   Battalion was re-organised into three companies.
In Bde Reserve Q 11.b & Q 11 c

22nd   ------ ditto ------
On the night of the 22nd/23rd the Battalion moved up and took over line from R.1;d;90:05 to a point on the road 200ˣ N-W of Road junction R 1 c 55.50
Dispositions (No 2 Coy on the right
              (No 1 Coy on the left
              (No 3 Coy in Reserve

23rd   Battn was in position and in touch with units on flanks by 00.15. *White brassards issued as distinguishing mark & worn on left arm.*
AT ZERO (01.20) the Battalion moved forward to the attack under a creeping barrage
A Message from O.C. No 2 Coy timed 0200 arrived at Btn Hqrs at 0345 stating that No 2 Coy had crossed the RICHEMONT RIVER but had lost touch with the 21st Manchesters on their right. As no further messages were received, the Bn Intelligence Officer 2/Lt E.T.B. Shepherd was sent forward from Bn Hqrs at 0500 to find out and report on the situation on the left. A message from the I.O. timed 0540 arrived at Btn Hqrs at 0615 stating that O.C. No 3 Coy with about 100 O.R. were on Sunken Road about 300ˣ N.E. of RICHMONT RIVER from R.1.a.08 to R.2.a 5.8. had reorganised and were moving forward.
At about 0700 owing to the obscurity of the situation and by the approval of the Brigadier who was at Btn Hqrs O.C. Btn left Headquarters and proceeded to POMMEREUIL. On arrival he found that the Battalion was being withdrawn from the 1st objective (RED LINE) into Bde Reserve near the CEMETERY L 32 d 9.7 by order of Major MURRAY (O.C. 21st Manchester Regt) who had taken over Command of the Bde front line. The positions of the Coys of the Btn previous to this was as follows:-
2/Lt R COX (No 2 Coy) with two Platoons of No 2 Coy and about 15 men of 21st Manchesters had dug in along the line of the 1st objective on the frontage of the right Btn of the Bde (21st Manchesters front) This party had arrived at POMMEREUIL with our barrage and was clearing the village when a Tank arrived which in the dark probably mistook them for the enemy. The tank however was warned and the village was mopped up, about 70 prisoners being taken.
2/Lt R COX and his party then advanced on to the 1st Objective with the barrage as above.
2/Lt Griffin with one Platoon of No 1 Coy arrived immediately in rear of the above mentioned tank, and also dug in on 1st Objective on the left of 2/Lt Cox.

contd.

continued. 2

Later on various parties of Devons and Manchesters who had become mixed during the darkness and also parties who had been temporarily held up by enemy M.Gs in vicinity of GARDE MILL arrived. One platoon of No 3 Coy was also on objective on the frontage of the left Bn of the Bde (20th Manchesters)

The Battalion accordingly re-organised in vicinity of the Cemetery and remained there until 1800 when it moved according to orders, via FORRESTERS HOUSE (L 27/d/6/9) and took up a position forming a defensive flank from L 33 d 5.3 to L 29.a.4.8. and consolidated in depth.
The same night (night of 23rd/24th) the Battalion was relieved at 0500 by the 1st Leinster. Estimated number of Prisoners taken during the day 150. A large number of M.Gs and many T.Ms and 77 mm Gun and several anti-tank guns were captured.

24th The Battalion returned to billets in POMMEREUIL where it was at one hours notice from midday. At 1800 the Btn left POMMEREUIL and relieved the 11th Sherwood Foresters in the front line near FONTAIN AU BOIS from G8 d 4.5. to G 2 d 2.1. Relief complete 2300.
Patrols were sent out during the night 24/25th

25th During the day the front held by the Btn was re-organised and posts pushed forward to concealed positions in the hedges
On the night of 25th/26th Patrols searched area 300ˣ to 400ˣ in front of our posts, one enemy post only being located within this area.

26th Throughout the day, daylight patrols reconnoitred in front of our line and located three enemy positions in addition to posts located yesterday.
On the night of 26th/27th the Battalion ordered to extend to the left and take over about 500ˣ from the 20th Manchesters Btn Frontage now extends from G.8d 4.5. to G 2d 2 3

27th Holding Line
28th Ditto   Col. Storey D.S.O. reassumed command of the Bn. in the afternoon. vice Capt. Pridham.
29th Ditto
30th aDitto
On the night of 30th/31st the Battalion was relieved by 7th Wilts.

SGD R.P. PRIDHAM Captn
for Lieutenant Colonel
31/10/18   Cmdg 9th (S) Battalion The Devonshire Regiment

NOTE. During the operations one of the most noticable features was that Officers who used their compasses reached the objective with the barrage with little loss of direction. The value of the use of the compass, even in daytime in enclosed country cannot be too strongly inferred upon all Officers and N.C.Os.

Casualties	Officers	O.R.	Total
Killed	2Lt.R.P.YEATMAN 23/10/18 2/Lt.M.W.HIGGS 23/10/18	10	2 Offs. and 10. O.R.
Wounded	—	80	80. O.R.
Missing	2Lt.W.J.HYATT 25/10/18 (believed killed)	2	1 Off and 2. O.R.

Army Form C. 2118.

9th (Ser) BATTALION THE DEVONSHIRE REGIMENT
WAR DIARY
INTELLIGENCE SUMMARY
(Erase heading not required)

NOVEMBER 1918.

Instructions regarding War Diaries and Intelligence Summaries are contained in F. S. Regs., Part II. and the Staff Manual respectively. Title pages will be prepared in manuscript.

Place	Date	Hour	Summary of Events and Information	Remarks and references to Appendices
LE CATEAU	1st.		Battalion in billets. Companies at disposal of O.C. Coys for general cleaning up. 2/LT.R.F.B. DOBLE & LIEUT.C.H.BROCK joined for duty. 58 Other ranks reinforcements, joined Battalion. 2/LT.J.H.BRAUND & 2/LT.A. EDE joined Battalion for duty.	
"	2nd.		Battalion in billets. Companies at disposal of O.C. Coys for training of specialists. MAJOR.D.N.BRUNICARDI.M.C. (R.W.F. att'd) & Lieut.H.C.WILSON REjoined Battalion from Hospital. 155 Other Ranks Reinforcements joined.	
LE CATEAU	3rd.		Battalion marched to POMMEREUIL at 1545 and bivouacked on East Side of village. Four casualties on the road. Brigade in Reserve.Major.D.N. BRUNICARDI,M.C. attached to H.Q. 7th Infantry Brigade. Capt.R.O.SCHUH.M.C. to Hospital,Sick. when he said he go sick	
POMMEREUIL	4th.		Battalion 'standing to' under 15 minutes notice from Zero plus three (0945). Orders were received to move forward to MARLGARANI. Battalion marched off at 1448 hours. On the lines of march orders were received to take over an outpost line East of LANDRECIES	
	5th.		See narrative	
	6th.		See narrative	
	7th.		Battalion marched to LANDRECIES moving off at 1015.	
	8th.		See narrative period 3/8.11.18. 2/LT.G.H.HALL & 2/LT.E.I.MURRAY joined for duty. 2/Lt W.McALLISTER joined for duty	
LANDRECIES.	9th.		Companies at disposal of O.C. Companies for thorough cleaning up, Inspections of Arms and equipment etc. The following Honours were awarded to N.C.Os & Men of Battalion for conspicuous gallantry and devotion to duty during recent operations. Continued..	

Army Form C. 2118.

WAR DIARY
or
INTELLIGENCE SUMMARY

(Erase heading not required.)

Instructions regarding War Diaries and Intelligence Summaries are contained in F.S. Regs., Part II and the Staff Manual respectively. Title pages will be prepared in manuscript.

9/DEVON REGT.   NOVEMBER 1918 Contd.

Place	Date	Hour	Summary of Events and Information	Remarks and references to Appendices
LANDRECIES	9th (Contd)		The Corps Commander has, under authority granted by His Majesty the King, awarded the MILITARY MEDAL or Bar to same, to the u/m for conspicuous gallantry and devotion to duty during the recent operations, and congratulates them.	
			20738 Pte. J.FHOOPER. 267286 Pte J. VIGG.	
			10091 Pte. N. COURTNEY. 16462 Pte G. ATTIS.	
			66809 Pte.H.A.BRICE. 25824 Sgt W. PIKE.MM (Bar to MM	
			42663 L/C S.A.J.MEAGER. 13814 Sgt F. WOOD.	
			33538 Pte J. OSMOND. 16012 Cpl.C. COCKRAM	
			38092 L/C H. WHITE 33143 L/S E. DeAth.	
LANDRECIES	10th		Voluntary Church of England Service in Theatre at 1000. Working parties employed on cleaning up billets. 105 Other ranks reinforcements joined Battalion.	
LANDRECIES	11th		Battalion reorganized on four Company basis. Two Companies employed on road maintenance,remaining two Coys at disposal of O.C. Companies for training.	
LANDRECIES	12th		Two Companies at disposal of O.C. Coys for training, two Companies employed on road maintenance between POMMEREUIL & LANDRECIES.	
LANDRECIES	13th		Orders received at 0100 hours to march to POMEREUIL. The Battalion moved off at 1030 and were correctly billetd in POMMEREUIL at 1400.hours. MAJOR.D.N.BRUNICARDI.M.C. proceeded on Leave to U.K., CAPT.R.F..PRIDHAM.M.C. assumed duties as second-in-Command of Battalion.	
POMMEREUIL	14th		Companies at disposal of O.C. Companies for general cleaning up kit Inspections etc. Medical Officer's Inspection of men in billets.	
POMMEREUIL	15th		Company drill, P.T. and musketry. One Company employed on clearing road and billets.	

Army Form C. 2118.

WAR DIARY
or
INTELLIGENCE SUMMARY.
(Erase heading not required.)

Instructions regarding War Diaries and Intelligence Summaries are contained in F. S. Regs., Part II. and the Staff Manual respectively. Title pages will be prepared in manuscript.

Place	Date	Hour	Summary of Events and Information	Remarks and references to Appendices
POMMEREUIL	16th.		Company drill, P.T., Musketry &:Saluting drill. One Company employed cleaning up billeting area and road maintenance. All Officers of Division attended a tea with concert by Divisional Pierrottes at LE CATEAU at invitation of Divisional General.	
POMMEREUIL	17th.		Voluntary Church of England Service 1045 Holy Communion 1045 in Concert Room on BASUEL Road.	
POMMEREUIL	18th.		Battalion parade for Route march at 0915.FONTAINE AU BOIS to MALGARNI. Half Company employed in billets cleaning up. Commanding Officer inspected transport.	
POMMEREUIL	19th.		Company drill, P.T. Musketry etc. One Company employed on road maintenance. Two Companies on salvage work on area N.W. of Village, working towards FOREST. LT.R.P.C.HARVEY.M.C. & 2/LT.F.HOARE joined for duty. LT.HARVEY assumes Command of No.1.Company.	
POMMEREUIL	20th		Two Companies employed on Salvage work in Battalion salvage area. One half Company working in village cleaning up and road maintenance. Battalion blankets put thro' Foden disinfector.	
POMMEREUIL	21st.		Three Companies on salvage work on Battalion salvage area. One Company employed in billeting area cleaning up and road maintenance.	
POMMEREUIL	22nd.		Two Companies on salvage work in Battalion salvage area. One Company in billeting area cleaning up etc. One Company training,Coy drill etc.	
POMMEREUIL	23rd.		Two Companies on salvage work on Battalion salvage area. One Company in village cleaning up etc. One Company training, Company drill etc. Signalling class commenced	
POMMEREUIL	24th.		Voluntary Church of England Service at 1100. G.O.C. 7th Infantry Brigade inspected Regimental transport at 1015. Battalion half company football competition commenced. contd	

Army Form C. 2118.

WAR DIARY
or
INTELLIGENCE SUMMARY

9th DEVON REGIMENT. - NOVEMBER 1918. (Erase heading not required.)

Place	Date	Hour	Summary of Events and Information	Remarks and references to Appendices
POMMEREUIL	25th		Two Companies on salvage work on Battalion salvage area. One Company Training. Instruction of signallers. One Company cleaning billeting area and roads maintenance.	
POMMEREUIL	26th		Two Companies on Salvage work on Battalion Salvage area. One Coy training. Instruction of signallers. One Company clearing billeting area and road maintenance.	
POMMEREUIL	27th		Three Companies on Salvage work on Battalion salvage area. Baths at POMMEREUIL allotted to No.2.Company from 0930 to 1230.	
POMMEREUIL	28th		The whole Battalion on Battalion salvage area.	
POMMEREUIL	29th		Battalion move by march route to QUIEVY, moved off at 1000 and arrived in billets at 1430. The following Honours were awarded to the u/m Officers, N.C.O.s and men for conspicuous gallantry and devotion to duty during recent operations. The Field Marshal Commanding in chief has, under authority granted by His Majesty the King, awarded the following decorations. BAR TO THE DISTINGUISHED SERVICE ORDER. Major (T/Lt.Col.) H.I. STOREY.,D.S.O. BAR TO THE MILITARY CROSS. 2/LT. (A/Capt) R.O. SCHUH.M.C. THE MILITARY CROSS. 2/LT.W.E.MANLEY. THE DISTINGUISHED CONDUCT MEDAL. 12505 Cpl. H.E. PEARSON. 14449 Cpl. T. PHELPS. Contd....	

Army Form C. 2118.

WAR DIARY
or
INTELLIGENCE SUMMARY

9th DEVON REGT. NOVEMBER 1918

Place	Date	Hour	Summary of Events and Information	Remarks and references to Appendices
POMMEREUIL	29th Contd.		**Honours & Awards Contd.** The Corps Commander has, under authority granted by His Majesty the King, awarded MILITARY MEDALS to the following N.C.Os & Men.	
			#57322 L/C J.P. MATTHEWS,D.C.M. 14340 Sgt. S.J. HARPER.	
			9458 Pte C. TUCKERMAN. 31547 Pte H.E. BAKER.	
			15807 Pte W. NEWMAN 31491 Pte A. EAMER.	
			23157 Pte H.C. VENNING. 31753 Cpl D. ROBERTS.	
			43234 Pte T. RADMORE.	
QUIEVY	30th		Companies at disposal of O.C. Companies for thorough cleaning of billets.	
			Strength of Battalion 30/11/18. Officers..40. Other Ranks.760.	
			Casualties during month.Killed....Offrs. 0.Other Ranks 3.	
			Wounded.... " 1 " " 27.	
			" 1 30.	
			Other Ranks admitted to Hospl Sick during Month = 46.	

Lt. Colonel.
Commanding 9th (S) Battn. The Devonshire Regiment.

9th (Ser) Battalion The Devonshire Regiment.

Narrative of Operations from 3rd to 8th November 1918.

3rd. Novr.   The Battalion marched from LE CATEAU at 1545 to POMMEREUIL where it bivouaced for the night with the rest of the Brigade. 4 Other ranks were wounded on the march by shell fire.

Orders for operations for the 4th were received and Battalion warned to be prepared to move at 15 mins notice from 0915 4th.

4th.   Battalion prepared to move from 0915 - orders to move received at 1400 - Battalion moved off ~~from~~ for MALGARNI at 1448. During the march orders were received that the Battalion would take up an out post position on "Red Line" (E. of LANDRECIES) These orders were issued to Companies at 1635 & Battalion moved off at 1640.

The Battalion crossed SAMBRE CANAL by trestle foot bridge near lock and the line was occupied by all three Companies on outpost by 2300 17 casualties were caused (all by one shell) One Officer killed in morning. During the night orders were received that the Brigade were to be prepared to move at 0730 the 5th.

LT BROOK

5th.   At 0920 B.M.531 - timed 0810 was received stating that the Battalion was to concentrate near the main road and be prepared to move at 15 minutes notice. Orders for move received at 1045, Battalion joined column at 1130. The Battalion moved to MAROILLES where it dug in for the night.

6th.   The Battalion moved off at 0615 as head of the main body - the 20th Manchesters finding the advanced guard - after the 20th Manchesters had ~~forced~~ forced the passage of the GRANDE HELPE RIVER the 9th Devons moved to TAISNIERES at 1250 and crossed river by pontoon bridge at 1500 and took up defensive position E of LES CATTIAUX - after 20th Manchesters had taken DOMPIERRE. The Battalion moved into billets in LES CATTIAUX at 2300.

7th.   The advance was resumed at 0715 - 21st Manchesters finding advanced guard, 9th Devons head of main body. The advance was slow at the beginning owing to fog which was very thick, the advance however proceeded as far as LES TUILIERES farm where it was held up by M.G. fire.

At 1500 9th Devons sent out patrol to get into touch with the 75th Brigade on right - which they succeeded in doing, finding the 6th Gloucesters in ST. HILAIRE.

Orders received at 1305 that advance was to cease at 1630 and Battalion to get into billets - which it did in vicinity of J.3.c.9.1 at 1800. It was relieved by 6th Lanc Fusiliers at 2200 - and then returned to billets in DOMPIERRE.

8th.   Battalion moved at 1015 to LANDRECIES where it was billeted by 1430.

Lt.Col.

HQ in town Pn bo I5c.4.6.
Our line is a ridge I5a - I5c
Enemy has dug in a ridge
I5d have sent platoon
to outflank him if poss.
In atck 50Dn on left
X flank in Au
Please take necessary
precautions

W.24. 6. 1500.
───
Devon Cᵘ forward
in I.4.d
HQ I.3.b n.0.

9th Devon Regt.

Narrative of Operations from
3rd to 8th Nov. 1918.

3rd Nov. The Battn marched from LE CATEAU at 15.45 to POMMEREUIL where it bivouacked for the night with the rest of the Bgde. 4 O.R. were wounded on the march by shell fire.

Orders for operations for the 4th were received & Batt was warned to be prepared to move at 15 min notice from 09.15 a.m.

4th. Batt prepared to move from 0915. Orders to move received at 12.00 - Batt moved off for MALGARNI at 14.48.

During the march orders were received that the Battn would take up an Outpost position on "Red Line" (E of LANDRECIES). These orders were issued to Coy's at 16.35 & Battn moved off at 16.40.

The Battn crossed by trestle foot bridge near lock, & the

line was occupied by all 3 Coys. on Outpost by 2300 — 17 casualties were caused (all by one shell) — 1 Off. killed in morning.

During the night orders were received that the Bgde. were to be prepared to move at 07.30 the 5th.

5th. At 09.20 B.M. 531 — timed 0810 was received, stating that the Battn was to concentrate near the main road & be prepared to move at 15 min. notice. Orders for move received at 10.45 Battn joined column at 1130. The Battn moved to MAROILLES where it dug in for the night.

6th. The Battn moved off at 0645 as head of the main body. the 20th Manchesters finding the advanced guard — after the 20th Manchesters had forced the passage of the GRANDE HELPE RIVER. the 9th Devons moved to TAISNIERES at 1250 & crossed river by pontoon bridge at 1500 & took up defensive position E of LES CATTIAUX. After 20th Manchesters had taken DOMPIERRE the Battn

moved into billets in LES
CATTIAUX at 2300.

7th The advance was resumed
at 0715. 21st Manchesters
finding advanced guard
9th Devons head of main
body. The advance was
slow at the beginning owing
to fog. which was very
thick — the advance however
proceeded as far as LES TUILIERES
farm where it was held
up by M.G. fire.
 At 1300 9th Devons sent out
patrol to get into touch with
the 75th Bgde on right —
which they succeeded in
doing — finding the 6th Gloucesters
in ST HILAIRE.
 Orders received at 1305 that
advance was to cease at
1630 & battⁿ to get into
billets — which it did in
vicinity of J.3.C.9½ at 1800
 It was relieved by 6th Lanc⁵
Fusiliers at 2200 — & then
returned to billets in DOMPIERRE

8th Battⁿ moved at 10.15 to LANDRICIES
where it was billeted by 1430

16/11/18.
H. Stroyfter
Comdg 9th Devons

Secret

Instructions for advance on 6/11/18

Ref. Map 57a. 1/40,000.

6 Nov. 1918.

1/ 25th Div'n will continue advance to-day on a Two-Brigade front.
74 Inf Bde will be on Right and 7 Inf Bde on Left.

2/ Boundaries 7 Inf Bde.
Northern Bdy. will be prolongation of Divl Northern Bdy.
Southern Bdy. due East from H.17. Central to J.7 Central
Stream in I.10. inclusive to 7th Inf Bde.

3/ Objective due East from Cross Roads at HUNNOMAM. J.7.b.2.0 to Cross Roads at J.2.a.2.5. (both inclusive)

4/ Line of Advance - MAROILLES. Cross Rds H.11.c.4.4. - BASSE NOYELLES - I.8.a.0.7

2/

H.Conts/

- Road Junction I.2.d.9.3 — I.3.b.5.1
- I.1? Central.

5/ Advanced Guard to 7 Inf Bde will consist of
    20th Manchester Leah
    1 Troop 17th Lancers.
    1 Section 105 Fld Coy RE
Advanced Guard will pass RUE DES HAIES (H.6.c.0.0.) at 0630 hours

6/ Provides that Advanced Guard passes through Outpost line held by B" without a check. Coys will concentrate as under:
    HQ Coy and C Coy at H.b.d 50.99.
    B. D. & A Coys at H.b.b 90.10.
Unless orders are received to the contrary these concentrations will be completed by 0710 hours.

3/

7/ Order of March – Main Body.

9th Devon Regt.
21st Manchester Regt.
– Coy 25th Bn M.G.C
105 Fld Coy R.E.
150th Bde R.F.A.

8/ Bn will move in following Order
HQ. C – B – D – A. Coys
Reports to Head of HQ Coy
50x lateral will be maintained between
Platoons.

9/ ACKNOWLEDGE.

Issued at 0105 by runner

Gustavas Lt Colonel

9(S) Bn The Devonshire Regt.
Dec 1918.

WAR DIARY
or
INTELLIGENCE SUMMARY.
(Erase heading not required.)

Army Form C. 2118.

Place	Date	Hour	Summary of Events and Information	Remarks and references to Appendices
QUIGNY	1st.		There were Parade services for men of the following denominations C of E, R.C. of England, Roman Catholic, Presbyterians & Wesleyans.	
"	2nd		As the Battalion had only recently arrived in the village work consisted of a general cleaning up of Billeting area.	
	3rd		There were Two Companies engaged on Salvage work and Two Companies Training. Lewis gun classes were carried on. In the afternoon the first game of Battalion cricket - by football Competition (association) was played between B/1 Coy & 3. & B. 2 Coy. O. Education Classes were started.	
	4th		Owing to the visit of His Majesty the King there was no salvage work done but orders were received up to 10.0 A.m. as weather conditions would not admit of it. The Battalion formed up on either side of the QUIGNY-BEVILLERS Road about 100 yards East of QUIGNY. 30° Infantry formation was adopted. At 13.30 His Majesty arrived by motor accompanied by the Prince of Wales. His Majesty walked through the Brigade group and His Majesty's left Army. Two Companies were again engaged on Salvage work and Two Coys Training.	
	5th		Owing to His Majesty's visit the preceding day the second game of the Battalion Competition was not played. The place in the afternoon was played between H.Q. & 3 & B Coy v. No. 1 Coy 4. 1 Coy D. 1st Coy 2 No. 1 Coy 2 & Infection was received of death through sickness of Cpln. a.b.t. Rattan, "C" Coy	
	6th		Two Coys again engaged on Salvage work. Two Coys Training. In the afternoon the Final of Battalion football Competition was played.	
	7th		The Divisional General Major Gen. L.G. CHARLES C.B. CSS Presented Medal ribbons and widow at a Divisional Parade held East of BOUSSIÈRES STRAIGNE BEVILLERS AVESNES Cross Roads. A representative Company of Line Officers and one hundred Other Ranks from each Brigade attended.	39 D

WAR DIARY
or
INTELLIGENCE SUMMARY
(Erase heading not required.)

Army Form C. 2118.

Place	Date	Hour	Summary of Events and Information	Remarks and references to Appendices
QUIEVY	7th		Capt A.J.F. PRYNNE was in Command of Bde. Infantry Brigade Hdqrs. The undermentioned received their medal ribbons since Bars.	
			Lt. Col. H.T. STOREY DSO a Bar to Distinguished Service Order	
			42663 Pte Ct. Hagen Military Medal	
			13628 Pte A. Osmond " "	
			38092 Pte W. Stile " "	
			16012 Sgt C. Cockram " "	
			20438 Pte F.T. Horton " "	
			Salvage work was carried out by all Coys in their respective Hutting areas in the afternoon the first round of Brigade Inter Coy Football Competition was played the competition was on the knock out system. Return winning Company teams of Battalions D & C.Coy. Reserve 7th & Coy H 25th D & C Coy.	
	8th		There were services for men of the following denominations. Church of England, Roman Catholic, Presbyterians and Wesleyans. In the afternoon the Officers played the Sergeants at Soccer. Result Officers 3 Sergts 0.	
			The Cinema at QUIEVY opened.	
	9th		There was another Divisional Parade for the presentation of medal ribbons. One Section and 2nd other ranks represented the Battalion in the Brigade representative Coy. The following men received their medal ribbons.	
			14728 Sgt C.C. Matthews D.C.M. Military Medal	
			14340 " G. Harper " "	
			13807 Pte R.F. Newman " "	
			514753 " D. Colbert " "	
			432344 " L. Gatmore " "	
			Leap Coys were on Salvage work, wire Coys Cleaning.	

Army Form C. 2118.

WAR DIARY
or
INTELLIGENCE SUMMARY.
(Erase heading not required.)

Instructions regarding War Diaries and Intelligence Summaries are contained in F. S. Regs., Part II. and the Staff Manual respectively. Title pages will be prepared in manuscript.

Place	Date	Hour	Summary of Events and Information	Remarks and references to Appendices
QUIEVY	9th		Route. In addition the Medical Officer held an inspection of all C.B.'s and men for lice and scabies, the inspection was held in relation for the Divisional Baths. 2/Lt Capt GRIFFIN reported from Hospital 2/Lt F.F. BONNIWELL and 2/Lt J.F. BRODIE R.A. joined for duty. A Scotland class was started.	
	10th		Two Coys on Salvage and 100 Boys training. 5 "cal Marius" proceeded to CAMBRAI for interview, prior to their detail to Cologne. A Commercial Correspondence class was started.	
	11th		Two Coys on Salvage and Two Coys training 100 Boys training at Div 6 Socca Ground. The Pioneer Bat 11 of 33th Bn. & Lot James Regt at Socca Ground. 2 Lemons J. 11 & Lot James O.	
	12th		Two Companies on Battalion Salvage area & 100 Boys training. Walkers-nous dockilites to England or Demobilize. Same ofcbatalion on Lice. Two Boys on Salvage & Two Boys training.	
	13th		A lecture of mathematics was delivered. Two Coys on Salvage work and 100 Boys training. Practise game of Rugby was played "C" Coy versus Rest of Batn. Rest 19. Lot Caps N1K.	
	14th		6 Others were Lance Corporal Services for men of the following denominations church of England, Roman Catholic, Presbyterian & Wesleyans. Two Coys on Salvage area & 100 Boys training.	
	15th		Preparations were made for a collecting wood for fires & lighting Company lighting rooms.	
	16th		The Battalion was allotted to Divisional Baths at AVESNES LES AUBERT The Battalion blankets and all S.D. including greatcoats were disinfected. No Salvage parties went out except conducting parties for the Lagons. There was a little snow in Bivouacs Areas.	
	17th		There were 88 entries. Lt. F.K. HUGHES joined for duty.	

A6945 Wt. W1422/M1160 350,000 12/16 D. D. & L. Forms/C/2118/14.

WAR DIARY
or
INTELLIGENCE SUMMARY

Army Form C. 2118.

(Erase heading not required.)

Place	Date	Hour	Summary of Events and Information	Remarks and references to Appendices
QUIEVY	18th		Two Companies on Salvage work & two training. A draft class was started 29 miners proceeded to CAMBRAI for Colonial prior to being demobilized to U.K.	
	19th		Two Companies on Salvage work as done by roads & billeting area. Twelve Coys training.	
	20th		Two Coys on Battalion Salvage area. One Coy training work on roads & the field's continued.	
	21st		Three Coys on Salvage work. One Coy training work on roads and Rifle's continued. The Battn. Rugger 11thother James Soccer XI well. 11th Lanes 1 & Divrs 1.	
	22nd		Draught Tournament in Recreation Room 2nd entries. The following Divine Service. There were Parade service for men of the following Presbyterian denominations & went to England. Four Teams proceeded and Scotsman.	
	23rd		Two Coys on Salvage Area. Two Coys training to CAMBRAI for entraining prior to demobilize to U.K.	
	24th		Saw a holiday. Coys were occupied in preparing billets, being rooms etc for the Xmastime. Intentation and Coy Soccer games were Played. E Avolimos supplies were issued 1300 hrs. (Pte Bonet and Coy forty men met Belos Headquarters, Battn HQrs and Coy Messes.	
	25th		Divine Service, carol service for men of the following denominations (Church of England) Roman Catholics Presbyterians and Wesleyan's & Nicholas juniors were a great success. Beer York whiskey, pickles sence, Cigarettes being provided. Sergeons were held in the log during Room's after dinner. Tax in the morning for all mounted officers. So by there was a Horse Race at Belay by AMC on "Peggie" went in a holiday. The Battalion played the 166th RBy F.E at Rugby ils. AMC on "Peggie". The Battalion played the 166th RBy F.E 6 Diver's 0 at Base	
	26th		Boxing day was a holiday. 2 Cold Others departed to Base	

Army Form C. 2118.

WAR DIARY
or
INTELLIGENCE SUMMARY.
(Erase heading not required.)

Instructions regarding War Diaries and Intelligence Summaries are contained in F. S. Regs., Part II. and the Staff Manual respectively. Title pages will be prepared in manuscript.

Place	Date	Hour	Summary of Events and Information	Remarks and references to Appendices
QUIEVY	27th		Two Coys on Salvage work. Two Coys on Route March owing to a Pierrot performance at CAMBRAI to which the Battalion was proceeding by lorries being returned to Billets by 1130. Owing to the lack of lorries the performance was cancelled. But Evening Pierrots took a 2nd time was held in the Recreation Room at 1700 hours, there were 72 entries.	
	28th		Two Companies engaged on Salvage work, two Companies training	
	29th		Divine services for Church of England, Roman Catholics, Presbyterians and Wesleyans in the afternoon Officers & Drums played Officers " & six Lance Sergts 9 at Arras 2/11th L Lancs.C.	
	30th		The whole Battalion was engaged on Salvage work. Two Coys were being on Battalion area and two Coys clearing at 0950 hours at Church BETHENCOURT for work with 2/6 Bn Batt. Manchester Regt.	
2/12.			The whole Battalion was again engaged in salvage work. Two Companies working with 21st Manchesters. Six lorries took men from two Coys to CAMBRAI for a performance of the Pierrots Cough. (The Divisional Coucy.) leaving QUIEVY at 1230 hours delivering about 1445 hours the lorries then made a second journey taking men from other two Companies to a performance commencing at 2000 hours.	
			The Battalion gave a treat for the Children of QUIEVY in the evening commencing at 1700 hours. Several films were shown and a ventriloquist and an animal imitator also performed.	
			contd

WAR DIARY or INTELLIGENCE SUMMARY.

Army Form C. 2118.

(Erase heading not required.)

Summary of Events and Information

Classes. The following is list of subjects in which instruction was given, and the average attendance at each, for a month.

Average attendance.

| Sen⁴ Officers | 14 |
| | 14 |

The following were instructors:
- Lt Col Williams
- " Gale
- Lt Guissoni
- Rev C Foster
- " Nicholson G.E.

Spanish	9	Victoria Geography
English	3	Spanish
History	1	
Geography	4	Mathematics
Mathematics	4	Shorthand &
Carpentry	7	Com. corresp.
Shorthand	8	
Commercial Correspondence	10	Lawson G.E. English
		French

The areas reserved by the Battalion during the month were:

The triangle formed by the villages of BOUSSIERES, BEVILLERS, ST HILAIR triangle formed by S. corner of CARNIERES, FERME du FRESNOY and Rouse junction on East side of BEVILLERS.

Area S.W. of BEVILLERS formed by BEVILLERS – FOUR à CHAUX to farm at road junction 1500 yds N.W. of BEAVOIS.

Area from farm ½ mile N of BEAVOIS due East to Road Junction near ALLICOURT FERME thence South to Road Junction N of HARPIGNY FERME thence West of BEVILLERS.

Area bounded by South & East Junction of QUIEVY-AUDRY Roud and CAMBRAI Rd to HARPIGNY FME. On north by Road running East to Railway shown South to level crossing on CAMBRAI Road.

Casualties during month Capt A E NAPPIN M.C. piece of schrapnel 30/10/18
Other Ranks transferred to Y or List 744.

WAR DIARY
or
INTELLIGENCE SUMMARY.
(Erase heading not required.)

Army Form C. 2118.

Place	Date	Hour	Summary of Events and Information	Remarks and references to Appendices
			Officers serving with Battalion during month of December.	
			Lt Col A.J. Storey DSO	
			Major D.N. Blencowe MC	
			Captn R.O. Buckton MC	
			Captn F.S. Palmer "	
			Lieut R.P.C. Stanney MC	
			Captn at L. Guyone	
			Lieut L.G. Rogers 2/Lt E.L. Murray	
			Lieut G.a. Williams " G.H. Stee	
			Lieut A.D. Carey " C.y. Ellwood	
			Lieut A.C. Wilson " a.f. Coe	
			Lieut L.L. Bonniwell " G.H. Beaumer	
			Lieut L.L.L. Hughes " A.H.G. Smith MC	
			" " W. Lott " K.H. Blenkin Lpl. C. Holloway	
			" " F. Bishop " L.L. Potts 2/Lt T.L. Rhees	
			" " Pearce " a. Pearson	
			" C.I.B. Farmer " A.E. Thorley MC Lt Col Jacob (sick)	
			" A.H.Y. Taylor " G.H.B. Stone Le Da Belay	
			" E.J.B. Chr Allestie " L.a. Benjamin M.S.M.C.	
			" E.N. Lawrence " Roy Coe MC Medical Officer	
			" L.J. Stephens " L.J. Brodie R.E.	
			" " Bliss " Sgt Griffin	
			" A. Moore	
			A.J. Grice L.S. McCormick	

Cmdg (S) Bn. the Devonshire Regiment.

Army Form C. 2118.

WAR DIARY
or
INTELLIGENCE SUMMARY.

(Erase heading not required.)

Army Form C. 2118.

1st Devon
Vol 40

40 D.

Instructions regarding War Diaries and Intelligence Summaries are contained in F. S. Regs., Part II. and the Staff Manual respectively. Title pages will be prepared in manuscript.

BATTALION ~~1st Devon~~ JANUARY 1919.

Place	Date	Hour	Summary of Events and Information	Remarks and references to Appendices
QUIEVY	1		The Whole Battalion was on Salvage. Two Companies working on 21st Manchester Rest Area. Lorries conveyed men from two Companies to Divisional Flareots at CAMBRAI at 1400 hours. The lorries made a second journey at 1800 hours to convey men who were unable to go previously.	
QUIEVY	2		The Whole Battalion on Battalion Salvage Area.	
QUIEVY	3		The Battalion marched to ENGLEFONTAINE, on the borders of FORET de MORMAL. Starting at 0825 hours halted at 1250 hours at a point midway between VENDEGIES & PONT DU NORD for dinners. The Battalion was correctly billeted at 1545 hours. Falling out etc. NIL.	
ENGLEFONTAINE	4		The Billets were poor, village having been heavily shelled. Lt.Col. H.I. STOREY, D.S.O. assumed Command of 7th Infantry Brigade vice Brig.Gen.HICKIE on leave. MAJOR D.H. BRUNICARDI M.C. assumed Command of Battalion.	
ENGLEFONTAINE	5H		Companies were engaged in cleaning up their billets, and doing such repairs as were possible.	
"	6S		There were Parade Services for men of the following religions - Church of England, Roman Catholics, Presbyterians, Wesleyans etc.	
"	7M		Companies were at disposal of O.C. Companies for general cleaning up of billets and Company billeting areas.	
"	8T		Companies at disposal of O.C Companies for general cleaning of billets and Roads.	
"	8		Two Companies were engaged on Salvage work inside the village, whilst the remaining Companies less one platoon were engaged on Ceremonial Training. One platoon was engaged on Road cleaning. The Divisional Commander inspected Salvage work & some of the Company billets during the morning. In the afternoon the Battn. played 132 Labour Coy at Soccer. Result. 8th Devon..11 132 Labour Corps 2	

A.C.O.)1. Wt. W1422/M160. 350,000. 12/16. D.D.& L. Forms/C2118/14.

Army Form C. 2118.

WAR DIARY
or
INTELLIGENCE SUMMARY.
(Erase heading not required.)

9th Devon Regt.   JANUARY 1919 Contd.

Place	Date	Hour	Summary of Events and Information	Remarks and references to Appendices
ENGLEFONTAINE	9		The Battalion was allotted the Divisional Baths at SALESCHES from 0800 to 1230 hours. On return of first Company, one platoon was engaged on road cleaning.	
"	10		Two Companies employed on Salvage work outside the village and two Companies on Ceremonial drill. One platoon road cleaning. Details went to baths SALESCHES at 1200 hours. There was a concert in the Patronage ENGLEFONTAINE given by "The Grousers" the concert party of the 132nd Labour Company. The following classes were discontinued owing to Instructor (Lieut.C.A.WILLIAMS) being admitted to Hospital. French (Officers), French (Other Ranks)	
"	11		Companies at disposal of O.C. Coys from 0800 to 1000. There was a Battalion parade at 1100 hours to practice the Ceremony of the Consecration & Trooping of the Colour. In the afternoon the Officers of the Battn. played N.C.O.s at soccer Result...Officers..4. N.C.Os....1.	
"	12		There were parade Services for men of the following denominations, Church of England, Roman Catholics, Nonconformists etc. In the afternoon the second round of Divisional "Enter-Battalion Cup (Soccer)" was played, the Battn playing 11th Sherwood Foresters at LOUVIGNIES. Result..9th Devon Regt...2. 11th Sherwood Foresters....2.	
"	13		The Battalion was engaged on Salvage from 0900 to 1230 hours. One platoon being engaged on road cleaning in the village. There were no parades in the afternoon owing to replay of match versus 11th Sherwood Fstrs. Result..9th Devon Regtrs...5. 11th Sherwood Frs...1. The following Officers were cross posted from 6th Dorset Regt and joined Battn for duty. 2/LT.J. BARRIDALE. 2/LT.F.J. PEARCE. 2/LT.G.F. RING, 2/LT.C.F. HITCHENS.	
"	14		Two Coys on ceremonial drill and two Coys on salvage, one platoon on road cleaning. One man admitted to Hospital with measles.	

Army Form C. 2118.

WAR DIARY
or
INTELLIGENCE SUMMARY.
(Erase heading not required.)

Instructions regarding War Diaries and Intelligence Summaries are contained in F. S. Regs., Part II. and the Staff Manual respectively. Title pages will be prepared in manuscript.

9th Devon Regt.   JANUARY 1919.

Place	Date	Hour	Summary of Events and Information	Remarks and references to Appendices
ENGLEFONTAINE	15		Companies were at disposal of O.C. Coys during the morning. At 1400 hours there was a Battalion parade to practice 'trooping the Colour'	
"	16		The four selected guards each consisting of 3 Officers and 64 Other Ranks paraded at 1000 hours for ceremonial drill. The remainder of Battalion was used as loading party for D.A.C. wagons and for general work on roads etc. In the afternoon the Third Round of the Divisional Inter Battalion Cup was played, the 1/8th Worcestershire Regt coming from CAMBRAI by lorry. Result...1/8th Worcesters..3. 9th Devon Regt...4. A Whist drive was held in 'The Patronage' there were 76 players.	
"	17		From 0900 to 1030 the selected Guards were at disposal of O.C. Guards on Battalion Parade ground. At 1100 The Battalion paraded for practice trooping the Colour. Loading parties for D.A.C. wagons were sent from men not required on ceremonial parade.	
"	18		Guards were at disposal of O.C. Guards for ceremonial drill until 1100 hours, when the Battalion paraded for ceremonial drill. In the afternoon the Officers of the Battalion played the Officers of the 11th Sherwood Foresters at LOUVIGNIES. Result...11th Sherwood Frs...3 9th Devon Regt...0.	
"	19		There were parade Services for men of the following denominations:- Church of England, Roman Catholics, Presbyterians Nonconformists etc. In the afternoon a sports meeting was held, the sports were arranged very hurriedly but were very successful.	

Army Form C. 2118.

WAR DIARY
or
INTELLIGENCE SUMMARY.

(Erase heading not required.) JANUARY 1919 Contd.

9th Devon Regt.

Place	Date	Hour	Summary of Events and Information	Remarks and references to Appendices
ENGLEFONTAINE	20		The Battalion was allotted the Baths at VENDEGIES. On return from Baths Companies were at disposal of O.C. Companies for remainder of the morning. At 1430 hours selected Guards paraded on Battalion parade Ground for Ceremonial Training. There was a Whist Drive at 'The Patronage' at 1750 hours. There were 76 players.	
"	21		The Battalion less one Platoon was on Salvage from 0900 to 1230 hours. At 1400 hours selected Guards paraded for ceremonial training.	
"	22		Guards were at disposal of O.C. Guards from 0900 - 1100. At 1130 hours the Battalion paraded for Ceremonial training. One in the afternoon the Battalion Soccer Team were taken by lorry to LOCQUINOL to play 12th Devon Regt (now 155 Labour Coy). Result..9th Devon Regt....4; 12th Devon Regt..1. The Pierrots were at POIX DU NORD, about 120 men attended performance at 1700.hrs. LT.COL. H.I. STOREY D.S.O. rejoined Battalion from 7th Infantry Brigade and re-assumed command of the Battalion.	
"	23		The whole Battalion was on Salvage work until 1500 hours, with the exception of two platoons who were engaged on road cleaning and general work around billets.	
"	24		The whole Battalion was on Salvage until 1230 hours. At 1430 the Battalion paraded on Battalion Parade ground for rehearsal of Trooping the Colour. There was a Whist drive at 1750 hours in the Patronage 64 players took part. Lt.F.F.BOWTHELL and 2/LT.F.C.B.PHILLIPS proceeded to CAMBRAI to rejoin there respective R.A.F. Squadrons in accordance with instructions received from 25th Division.	

Army Form C. 2118.

WAR DIARY
or
INTELLIGENCE SUMMARY.
(Erase heading not required.)

9th DEVON REGT.   JANUARY 1919 Cont'd.

Place	Date	Hour	Summary of Events and Information	Remarks and references to Appendices
ENGLEFONTAINE	25		bugcanies were at disposal of O.C. Coys from 0900 to 1050 hours. At 1100 hours Battalion paraded for a rehearsal of Trooping the Colour. At 1400 hours Battalion paraded for a second rehearsal of the ceremony. Owing to demobilisation of Pte OATES, instructor, the following classes were cancelled:- Arithmetic, Geography, Shorthand, History & English.	
"	26		There were parade Services for men of the following denominations, Church of England, & Roman Catholics. There were no other parades.	
"	27		At 1050. The Colour presented by His Majesty The King was consecrated by REVd JENKINS MC presented by MAJOR.GEN.J.R.E. CHARLES.,C.B,D.S.O. Commanding 25th Division, and Trooped 2/LT.W.E. MANLEY.M.C. received the Colour, after the march past and advance in Review Order, the Major General addressed the Battalion and complimented all ranks on the manner in which the march had been carried out, especially under the adverse weather conditions the ground being covered in snow. The words of the Major General were much appreciated by all ranks especially the reference to the actions at BEAUREVOIR, PONCHAUX and LANDRECIES and the fact that they were the first Battalion of the reformed 25th Division to go into action and also the first to make the break through the German lines which led to the final retreat and Armistice. The Battalion then marched past in fours headed by the Band and 'PETER' the regimental mascot (a German messenger dog captured at MAMETZ on the SOMME 1916. The Guards for the ceremony were constituted as follows:- Commanding Officer:- LT.CO. H.I. STOREY.D.S.O. Second in Command :- MAJOR. D.N. BRUNSKARDT.M.C. Adjutant :- CAPT. F.G. ROGERS. Regtl.Sergt.Major.- SERGT-MAJOR.W.MANLEY. No.1.Guard 50 men drawn in equal numbers from the oldest Soldiers in each Company under CAPT.R.P. FRIDHAM.M.C, LIEUT.R.C. WILSON 2/LT.W.E.D. MANLEY.M.C.,(Colour bearer) Cont'd.....	

Army Form C. 2118.

WAR DIARY
or
INTELLIGENCE SUMMARY.

8th DEVON REGT. JANUARY 1919, Contd.

(Erase heading not required.)

Place	Date	Hour	Summary of Events and Information	Remarks and references to Appendices
ENGLEFONTAINE	27		Trooping the Colour Contd.	
			No.2.Guard.	
			50 men under CAPT.J.W. PALMER, 2/LT.S de L JACOB, and 2/LT.W. SCOTT.	
			No.3.Guard.	
			50 men under LIEUT.R.P.C. HARVEY,M.C. 2/LT.G.F.J.P. STONE, and 2/LT.J.A. BENJAMIN.	
			No.4.Guard.	
			50 men under CAPT. A.J.F. PRYNNE. Lieut.H.D. CAREY and 2/LT.G.H.HALL.	
			Free beer was issued to the men and a free performance given for them at the STAR THEATRE POIX DU NORD by the Divisional Pierrots. The weather conditions made it impossible to hold the Battalion sports which had been arranged.	
"	28		Companies were allotted the baths at VENDEGIES from 0800 to 1830. On return from Baths Companies were at work on roads clearing snow etc.	
"	29		Owing to the snow and frost no salvage work could be done with the exception of clearing dumps. Two platoons were loading wagons with German ammunition for transporting to SALESCHES. The remainder of the Battalion were at disposal of O.C. Companies for work on roads etc in vicinity of billets. The baths at VENDEGIES were allotted to the Battalion from 1500 to 1630 hours, and all men who had not been previous day paraded at 1145 and marched to the Baths. In the afternoon a Brigade Transport show was held in Field North of POIX DU NORD ENGLEFON TAINE Road about midway between the two villages. The result of the Challenge Trophy was as follows:- Contd..	

WAR DIARY
or
INTELLIGENCE SUMMARY.

Army Form C. 2118.

(Erase heading not required.)

9th DEVON REGT. Summary of Events and Information JANUARY 1919.

Place	Date	Hour	Summary of Events and Information	Remarks and references to Appendices
ENGLEFONTAINE	29		BRIGADE TRANSPORT SHOW contd.	
			1st..9th Devon Regt........16 points.	
			2nd..21st Manchester Regt......13 points.	
			3rd..7th Infantry Brigade H.Q....9 points.	
			4th..20th Manchester Regt......8 points.	
			The following were the places gained by the Battalion representatives:-	
			Cooker......2nd Prize.	
			Watercart......1st Prize.	
			Pair.H.D. Horses......3rd Prize.	
			Pair.L.D. ......No place.	
			Mules......1st Prize.	
			Maltese Cart......3rd Prize.	
			Officers Chargers......3rd Prize.	
			Pack Mules......1st & 2nd Prizes.	
			The prizes were given to the winners by BRIG.GEN. G.I. HICKIE, Commdg 7th INF BDE	
			(Programme of events attached)	
"	30		Owing to the continuance of the cold weather no out salvage could be done, some work was done on dumps of German ammunition. Companies were at disposal of O.C. Coys for physical training, Route march or work on Roads.	
			A Whist tournament was held in the Patronage at 1750 hours. There were — players.	
"	31.		Parades were under Company arrangements. Work was done on the roads, the remainder of the men doing Physical training, Route marches etc. In the afternoon all animals of Y & Z classes were Mallein tested by the veterinary officer.	
			Contd......	

Army Form C. 2118.

WAR DIARY
or
INTELLIGENCE SUMMARY.

(Erase heading not required.)

9th Devon Regt. JANUARY 1918. Contd.

Place	Date	Hour	Summary of Events and Information	Remarks and references to Appendices
			The following Officers were serving with the Battalion during the Month.	
			Commanding Officer..Lt.Col.H.I. STOREY.D.S.O.	
			2nd in Command......MAJOR. D.N. BRUNICARDI;M.C.	
			Adjutant..........CAPT. F.G. ROGERS.	
			Capt. R.P. PRIDHAM.M.C. 2/LT.J.H. BRAUND.	
			Capt. J.W. PALMER. 2/LT.A.J. EDE.	
			Capt. A.J.F. PRYNNE. 2/LT.H.G. SMITH.	
			Lieut.R.P.G. HARVEY.M.C. 2/LT.J.H. BLACKLER.	
			Lieut.G.A. WILLIAMS. 2/LT.J.T. DOBBS.	
			Lieut.H.D. CAREY. 2/LT.C de L JACOB.	
			Lieut.H.C. WILSON. 2/LT.E. PEASGOOD.	
			Lieut.F.F. BONNIWELL. 2/LT.W.E. MANLEY.M.C.	
			Lieut.J.F.L. HUGHES. 2/LT.G.F.J.P. STONE.	
			2/LT. F.J. BISHOP. 2/LT.J.A. BENJAMIN.	
			2/LT.W. SCOTT. 2/LT. R. COX.M.C.	
			2/LT. W. PEARCE. 2/LT.J.F. BRODIE.	
			2/LT. C.S.R. FARMER. 2/LT.S.A.J. GRIFFIN.	
			2/LT. E.H.F. TAYLOR. 2/LT. G. HOLLOWAY.	
			2/LT. W. McALLISTER. 2/LT.F.C.B.PHILLIPS.	
			2/LT. R.J. TURNER. 2/LT.F.J. PEARCE.	
			2/LT. E.M.D. SHEPHERD. 2/LT.G.F. HUTCHENS.	
			2/LT. S.N. BLISS. 2/LT.G.F. RING.	
			2/LT. F. HOARE. 2/LT.J. BATTIBALL.	
			2/LT. E.I. MURRAY.	
			2/LT. G.H. HALL. Lt. & Q=Mr F.W. MAYNARD.	
			2/LT. E. ELLWOOD. Lt.W.A. PEISEY. U.S.A.M.C.	
			(Medical Officer)	
			=-=- Revd.E. FISHER.C.F. Chaplain.	
			Contd..	

Army Form C. 2118.

WAR DIARY
or
INTELLIGENCE SUMMARY.

(Erase heading not required.)

Place	Date	Hour	Summary of Events and Information	Remarks and references to Appendices
9th Devon Regt.			JANUARY 1919 Contd.	
			Area Salvaged during month as per attached sketch map.	
			Education Classes during the Month,:-	
			French (Officers)) discontinued 10/1/19 owing to Instructor French (Other Ranks)) (Lieut.C.A. WILLIAMS admitted to Hspl.	
			Arithmetic) Geography) discontinued 25/2/19 owing to demobilization Shorthand) of Instructor (Pte OATES) History) English)	
			During the Month the Cinema a POIX DU NORD was open nightly except from 22nd to 29th where the Pierrots gave performances.	
			Total number of men who proceeded for dispersal during the month on January was 110.	
			Strength of Battalion on 31/1/1919....45 Officers and 600 Other Ranks.	
			Number of Other Ranks admitted to Hospital during month..22.	
			[signature] Lt.Col. Commanding 9th (Service) Battalion THE DEVONSHIRE REGT.	

7th Infantry Brigade Transport Competition.

Event One. Officer's Rider. 3rd 15572 Pte FLETCHER. No 3 Coy.
Commanding Officer's Horse "Micky"

" 2. Cooker with horse, driver, and cook.
2nd No 2 Coy cooker. 290770 Pte Harris 2 Coy
21290 Pte Taylor. S. 2 Coy

" 3. Pack Animals.
1st 65550 Pte Davey No 2 Coy.
2nd 30035 Pte Finnemore No 2 Coy.

" 4. Water Cart with horse driver and water duty man
1st 31058 Pte Old No 2 Coy and
33715 Pte Street No 2 Coy.

" 5. One horse vehicle. Maltese cart.
3rd 290883 Pte Weeks No 2 Coy.

" 7. Pair light draught mules.
1st 31576 Pte Richards. No 3 Coy.

" 8. Pair Heavy draught horses.
3rd 12084 L/c Bryan No 1 Coy.

Challenge trophy.
1st 9th Devon Regt   16 points
2nd 21st Manchester Regt 13 "
3rd 7th Inf: Bde H.Qrs.   9 "
4th 20th Manchester Regt   8 "

7TH INFANTRY BRIGADE TRANSPORT COMPETITION.

1 copy

1. A Transport Competition for Battalions and Headquarters of 7th Infantry Brigade will be held half way between ENGLEFONTAINE and POIX DU NORD on Wednesday 29th January 1919.

2. The meeting will be held in a field duly marked as such. Judging will begin at 14.30 hours all entries being present by 14.00 hours.

3. The following is a list of events in the order of judging:-

No.1. <u>Officers Riders</u>. with groom and saddlery. *To be shown as ridden*
    1st Prize. 20 francs.   2nd Prize. 10 Francs.
             40   20

No.2. <u>Cooker</u> with horses, driver and one cook; all equipment to be complete.
    1st Prize. 20 Francs for Driver.   15 Francs for cook.
            40   30
    2nd Prize. 10 Francs for Driver.   5 Francs for cook.
            20   10

No.3. <u>Pack Animals</u>. with leader and saddlery complete (without Load)
    1st Prize. 20 Francs.   2nd Prize. 10 Francs.
            40   20

No.4. <u>Water Cart</u> with horse, driver and one water duty man. *Mules may be substituted for horses*
    Prizes as for cooker.

No.5. <u>One horse Vehicle</u> with horse and driver and long rein harness complete.
    1st Prize. 20 Francs.   2nd Prize. 10 Francs.
            40   20

No.6. <u>Pair Light Draft Horses</u> with driver and harness.
    1st Prize. 20 Francs.   2nd Prize. 10 Francs.
            40   20

No.7. <u>Pair Light Draft Mules</u> with driver and harness.
    Prizes as for Light Draft Horses.

No.8. <u>Pair Heavy Draft Horses</u> with driver and long rein harness complete.
    1st Prize. 20 Francs.   2nd Prize. 10 Francs.
            40   20

4. Points will be given for condition and grooming of animals, cleanliness and repair of harness, smartness, turn out of man and vehicle and points deducted for articles of equipment missing or defective. Points will not necessarily be given for new paint or varnish

5. Entries for any one event are limited to two per unit; competitions should be held where necessary by units.

eliminating

6. A Challenge Trophy value 150 Francs will be given to the unit gaining most points in the competition. Points will be counted as follows:-
    1st Prize. = 3 points.
    2nd Prize. = 2 "
    3rd *Place* = 1 "

7. It is hoped that four judges and a referee from outside the Brigade will consent to act, in which case it will be possible for events to be judged simultaneously.

8. The Entrance Fee will be 10 Francs in each case except for events No.2 and 4 which will be 10 Francs.

9. The following will act as officials:-
   (a) The Comittee - one officer from each Battn., the B.T.O. and an officer of the Brigade Staff.
   (b) Register Keeper - Lieut T.M.LEWIN.   7th Inf. Bde. H.Q.
   (c) Marshall - Sergeant F.WICKS.   R.A.V.C.
   (d) Judges - to be notified later.

10. The Committee will meet at Brigade Headquarters at 10.00 hrs. on 27th Jany. when representatives from Units will state number of entries and pay entrance fees.

W.T.Pidsley. Captain,
Brigade Major, 7th Infantry Brigade.

22/1/19.

9 Devon Rgt

41.D

WAR DIARY
or
INTELLIGENCE SUMMARY.

Army Form C. 2118.

(Erase heading not required.)

Place	Date	Hour	Summary of Events and Information	Remarks and references to Appendices
ENGLEFONTAINE	1-2-19		Companies were engaged in P.T. and recreational training. The horses and mules of the Battalion were taken to POIX DU NORD for inspection by the Veterinary Officer. The Foden disinfector was in use on three Companies' blankets.	
-"-	2		There were parade services for men of the following denominations: C.E., R.C.	
-"-	3		The Battalion was engaged on such salvage work as could be done, the weather being very bad, and baths at VENDEGIES were used by two Coys.	
-"-	4		The Battn was engaged on salvage work, recreational & physical training in the afternoon.	
-"-	5		A heavy fall of snow stopped salvage work, and the Battn had physical training and games. A good deal of work was done in repairs to billets, which added much to the comfort of the men. The baths at VENDEGIES were used by two Companies.	
-"-	6		Salvage work was in abeyance owing to the weather, and the Commanding Officer lectured the Battn on "the Army of Occupation and demobilisation."	
-"-	7		The Battn was engaged at drill and physical training	
-"-	8th		Little salvage could again be done, so recreational & physical training were engaged in. Lt. H. D'C. CAREY assumed command of "A" Coy vice Capt A.J.F. PRYNNE,	

Army Form C. 2118.

WAR DIARY
or
INTELLIGENCE SUMMARY.
(Erase heading not required.)

Instructions regarding War Diaries and Intelligence Summaries are contained in F. S. Regs., Part II. and the Staff Manual respectively. Title pages will be prepared in manuscript.

Place	Date	Hour	Summary of Events and Information	Remarks and references to Appendices
ENGLEFONTAINE	Feb 9th 1919		The following parade services were held; C. of E. 11:30 hrs, with a voluntary service at 18:00 hrs, and Holy Communion at 12:00 hrs. R.C., 09:00 hrs; and Nonconformists, 11:00 hrs.	
-"-	" 10th		The Battn. were engaged on drill & recreational training. It was notified that in future there would be no charge for admission to the Divisional Guests and Cinema.	
-"-	" 11th		The Divisional Baths were used by the Battalion. Two men proceeded on courses at the School of Cookery, ETAPLES. 2/Lt H.B. Smith, M.M. assumed duties of Educational Officer vice 2/Lt N. Pearce, on leave.	
-"-	" 12th		Companies were at disposal of O.C. Companies, all ranks proceeding on leave to the United Kingdom were warned against having money transactions with strangers. Several cases had recently occurred at railway stations in London of Bank of Engraving notes, which are easily mistaken for Bank of England notes, being proffered to soldiers in exchange for money.	
-"-	" 13th		The Battn. was engaged on salvage work, and also recreational and physical training. The baths at VENDIGIES were allotted to the Battn.	

Army Form C. 2118.

WAR DIARY
or
INTELLIGENCE SUMMARY.
(Erase heading not required.)

Place	Date	Hour	Summary of Events and Information	Remarks and references to Appendices
ENGLEFONTAINE	Feb 14-19		Battⁿ was engaged in salvage work. 2/Lt A. BRIDGWATER was awarded the Military Cross for conspicuous gallantry in action. (He was killed in action 8-10-18). 3/7556 Sergt J.H. Mailin awarded the Meritorious Service Medal for services in the field.	
- " -	" 15th		Companies were under the direction of O.C. Companies.	
- " -	" 16th		The following parade services were held: C. of E. 11.0 hrs; R.C. 0900 hrs; Nonconformists 10.30 hrs. A fire Picquet was detailed for the evening week. A G.R.O. (No 6241) was received asking for the return of field glasses and telescopes drawn to Officers & N.C.O.'s and not Return stating any instance in which they were found of special value.	
- " -	" 17th		Battⁿ was engaged in salvage operations	
- " -	" 18th		Companies at disposal of O.C. Coys. The Gambrai billeting party, under 2/Lt W Scott, proceeded at 10.0 hrs	
- " -	" 19th		The Battⁿ moved from ENGLEFONTAINE to CAMBRAI, proceeding as far as SOLESMES. The Colours were carried by 2/Lt J.A. Benjamin	

Army Form C. 2118.

WAR DIARY
or
INTELLIGENCE SUMMARY.
(Erase heading not required.)

Instructions regarding War Diaries and Intelligence Summaries are contained in F. S. Regs., Part II. and the Staff Manual respectively. Title pages will be prepared in manuscript.

Place	Date	Hour	Summary of Events and Information	Remarks and references to Appendices
SOLESMES	FEB 20		The Battn. continued the march to CAMBRAI (23 kilos) leaving SOLESMES at 0900 hrs, and reaching the Brigade starting point at ST. PYTHON at 1020 hrs. The Colours were carried by 2/Lt-S.J. Stone. The band, sadly depleted owing to demobilisation, rendered a good selection of music on the march. Cambrai was reached at 1730 hrs. Were the billets were found to be without window glass and badly damaged by shell fire. Falling out state: Nil.	
CAMBRAI	21st		Battn. engaged cleaning and repairing billets.	
"	22		Battn. again engaged cleaning and repairing billets. All men in the Army of Occupation warned to be held in readiness to proceed at two hours notice.	
"	23		The following parade services were held; C.of E., 1100 hrs at the Demobilisation Camp Theatre. R.C., 1000 hrs at Church of Louis. Nonconformist, 1045 hrs at 71st Field Ambulance.	
"	24		Companies were engaged cleaning and repairing billets.	
"	25th		The Battn. were on Physical training and cleaning billets.	
"	26		Major D.M. Dunwoodie M.C. assumed command of the	

Army Form C. 2118.

WAR DIARY
or
INTELLIGENCE SUMMARY.
(Erase heading not required.)

Place	Date	Hour	Summary of Events and Information	Remarks and references to Appendices
CAMBRAI	Feb. 26		Battalion, vice Lt-Col H.S. Toogood DSO on leave to U.K. The use of the phrase "In the Field" ordered to be discontinued in all official documents in which it has hitherto been used, and the actual name of the place inserted instead.	
"	27		The Battn. were under Bgd Grnds for kit inspection, the Battn at Rue de Belfort were allotted the Battn. The Battn were represented today by Lt R Coe M.C. + 2/Lt L Howe in the XIII Corps Rugger final between the 25th Division + the 46th Division. There was a large attendance of spectators, and the game resulted in a win for the 46th Division by 3 tries to nil. Subsequently Major Bush 25th Divl. Staff, presented a silver cup to each of the winning team, and a watch to the loser, as winners + runners-up respectively of the cup. Lt R.S.G. Harvey M.C. to be A/Capt whilst commanding a Company 7-11-18. A draft of 2 Officers (2/Lt E de L. Scott + 2/Lt J.H. Blacker) and 234 men were warned to parade tomorrow (march 1st) to proceed to the 1/5th 10 C.L.I. for the Army of Occupation.	
"	28		MISCELLANEOUS. Educational classes were discontinued on Feb 19 owing to instructors being demobilised. Battn. engaged on salvage work. Total number demobilised during the week:- Officers 2, Other ranks 205.	

Strength of Battn. 28-2-19 - Officers 41 O.R. 1158

B H Brunicardi Major
Comdg 9th (s) Bn Devon Regt

Army Form C. 2118.

WAR DIARY
or
INTELLIGENCE SUMMARY.
(Erase heading not required.)

2nd Devonshire Regt. February 1919 contd.

Summary of Events and Information

The following Officers were serving with the Battalion during the Month.

Commanding Officer Lt. Col. H.S. STOREY DSO
2nd in Command   Major P.W. BRUNICARDI MC
Adjutant   Capt. H.G. ROGERS

Capt.	R.P. PRIDHAM MC
Capt.	J.M. PALMER
Capt.	A.F. PRYNNE
2/Lt	R.P.C. HARLEY MC
2/Lt	H.D. CAREY
2/Lt	H.C. WILSON
2/Lt	F.E. BENNINGER
2/Lt	J.H. HUGHES
2/Lt	F.J. BISHOP
2/Lt	N. SCOTT
2/Lt	H. PEARCE
2/Lt	C.S.R. FARMER
2/Lt	R.H.F. TAYLOR
2/Lt	W. McALLISTER
2/Lt	R.J. TURNER
2/Lt	E.T.B. SHEPHERD
2/Lt	J.N. BLISS
2/Lt	F. MOARS
2/Lt	E.I. MURRAY
2/Lt	G.H. HALL
2/Lt	L. ELWOOD
2/Lt	J.H. BRAUND
2/Lt	H.G. SMITH
2/Lt	J.H. CHANDLER	2/Lt Gt PUG
2/Lt	A.T. DOBBS	2/Lt A.M.K.W. MAYNARD
2/Lt	C.A.L. JACOB	
2/Lt	A. PEARSON	Lt. W.R. BALSON USMMC (Medical Officer)
2/Lt	W.E. MANLEY MC	
2/Lt	J.P. STONE	Rev E. FISHER CF (Chaplain)
2/Lt	A. BENJAMIN	
2/Lt	R. COX MC	
2/Lt	J.F. BRODIE	
2/Lt	J.A.T. GRIFFIN	
2/Lt	A. HOLLOWAY	
2/Lt	F.J. PEARCE	
2/Lt	G.F. HITCHENS	

Contd

Army Form C. 2118.

WAR DIARY

(Erase heading not required.)

March 1919

Place	Date	Hour	Summary of Events and Information	Remarks and references to Appendices
CAMBRAI	1st March		At 1000 hours today a draft of two Officers(2/Lt C de L JACOB and 2/Lt J.H. BLACKLER and 234 men paraded to proceed to ETAPLES to join the 1/5th D.C.L.I. Regt under the Army of Occupation Scheme. The men were inspected by Major D.N. BRUNICARDI M.C. and wished the best of luck. Then headed by the Band marched to the Station where they entrained at 1100 hours but owing to circumstances over which the Battalion had no control did not steam out until 6 hours the next day. A Field Kitchen was sent to the Station to provide the men with hot meals during their long wait and reading material was also provided. Summer time came into use today;clocks being put forward 1 hour.	
CAMBRAI	2nd March		Voluntary Services were held at the English Church at 11hrs and 1830 hours and Holy Communion celebrated at 8 hrs the Roman Catholics at 10 hrs in the Church of St Louis and Nonconformists at 1045 hrs.,at the 76th Field Ambulance.	
CAMBRAI	3rd March		Owing to the Battalion being reduced to almost Cadre Strength there are on men available for parades, the majority being employed on Transport Work etc,. During the month the Baths at RUE DE BELFORT CAMBRAI were allotted to the Battalion on the 5th, 17th & 18th and 24th & 25th. The Following Special, was published. On relinquishing Command of the 25th Division I wish to thank all ranks for the Loyal manner in which they have co-operated with me during my tenure of command and especially during the months of October and November 1918 when this division took such a leading part in the operations which brought the war to a successful conclusion. The record of the 25th Division since it came to France in 1915 in one of which all of us must look back with the greatest pride including as it does a leading share in every major operation undertaken by the British Army in France in 1916 and 1917. In 1918 the Division withstood no less than 4 major attacks made by the Germans in their Great Offensive,and though its Infantry Battalions suffered to such an extent that they had to be replaced in "Toto" by units of other formations nevertheless the spirit of those Gallant Battalions survived,and inspired us who now form the Division to the victories	
March 8th CAMBRAI				

Army Form C. 2118.

WAR DIARY

~~INTELLIGENCE SUMMARY~~

(Erase heading not required.)

Instructions regarding War Diaries and Intelligence Summaries are contained in F. S. Regs., Part II. and the Staff Manual respectively. Title pages will be prepared in manuscript.

Place	Date	Hour	Summary of Events and Information	Remarks and references to Appendices
			in which we shared during the advance from BEAUEVOIR to beyond LANDRECIES. It is feelings with the deepest regret that I have now to say good-bye to the Gallant Officers and men who fought so well under me during this latter period, and in saying so I wish them the best of good luck in whatever walk of live their future may lead them. (Signed) J.R.E. CHARLES Major General Commanding 25th Division March 5th 1919 AVESNES LES AUBERT.	
CAMBRAI	March 15th		Lieut Col H.I. STOREY D.S.O. reassumes Command of Battalion on rejoining from leave 15/3/19.	
CAMBRAI	March 23rd		To celebrate the return of the 1st Regiment of Infantry(France) to CAMBRAI, who marched in on the 23rd after an absence of nearly 5 years, a review of the Regiment was held in the PLACE DES ARMES at 14 hrs. Invitations were extended to the Heads of the English Battalions in CAMBRAI and the Commanding Officers and Captain A.J.F. PRYNNE attended from this Battalion, after the march past the Regiment paraded the various streets of the town.	
			Total Number Demobilized during the Month Officers ......7........... Other Ranks ....11........... Re-enlisted Soldiers ..20.....	
			STRENGTH OF BATTALION 31/3/19.. Officers ....29.... Other Ranks ..101......	
			Number of Other Ranks admitted to Hospital during Month 4	

Army Form C. 2118.

WAR DIARY
or
INTELLIGENCE SUMMARY.
(Erase heading not required.)

Place	Date	Hour	Summary of Events and Information	Remarks and references to Appendices
CAMBRAI	March 27		The following Special Order was published. On leaving the XIII Corps I wish to express to G.O.C. and Staff Brigadiers, and all ranks of the Division, my hearty thanks for their loyalty and good work during their service in the Corps. I wish them all the best of luck in the future whether in the Army or in Civil Life. (Sgd) T.L.N. Morland Lieut General Commanding XIII Corps.	Contd

Instructions regarding War Diaries and Intelligence Summaries are contained in F. S. Regs., Part II. and the Staff Manual respectively. Title pages will be prepared in manuscript.

Army Form C. 2118.

WAR DIARY
or
INTELLIGENCE SUMMARY.
(Erase heading not required.)

Summary of Events and Information

The following Officers served with the Battalion during the Month

Commanding Officer Lieut Col H.I. STOREY D.S.O.
2nd in Command   Major   D.N. BRUNICARDI M.C.
Adjutant   2/Lieut   W.E. MANLEY M.C.

Captain R.P. PRIDHAM M.C.
Captain J.W. PALMER
Captain R.P.C. HARVEY M.C.
Captain A.J.F. PRYNNE
Lieut   H.D. CAREY
Lieut   H.C. WILSON
Lieut   F.F. BONNIWELL
Lieut   F.J.L. HUGHES
2/Lieut F.J. BISHOP
2/Lieut W   PEARCE
2/Lieut H.H.F. TAYLOR
2/Lieut W   MC ALLISTER
2/Lieut R.J. TURNER
2/Lieut E.T.B. SHEPHERD
2/Lieut S.N. BLISS
2/Lieut F   HOARE
2/Lieut E.I. MURRAY
2/Lieut L   ELLWOOD
2/Lieut J.H. BRAUND
2/Lieut H.G. SMITH
2/Lieut J.H. BLACKLER
2/Lieut J.T. DOBBS
2/Lieut C. de L JACOB

2/Lieut G.F.J.P. STONE
2/Lieut J.A. BENJAMIN
2/Lieut R   COX M.C
2/Lieut J.F. BRODIE
2/Lieut C   HOLLOWAY
2/Lieut F.J. PEARCE
2/Lieut G.F. HITCHENS

Lieut & Quartermaster
         E.W. MAYNARD

Revd E FISHER C.F. Chaplain

Contd

Army Form C. 2118.

WAR DIARY
or
INTELLIGENCE SUMMARY.
(Erase heading not required.)

The following Officers left the Battalion during the month for either demobilization or to join the Army of Occupation.

```
Lieut H.D. CAREY       for dispersal  13/3/19
2/Lieut C HOLLOWAY     for     "      15/3/19
2/Lieut J.T. DOBBS     for     "      15/3/19
2/Lieut W PEARCE       for     "      25/3/19
2/Lieut E.I. MURRAY    for     "         "
2/Lieut F.J. BISHOP    for     "         "
2/Lieut W McALLISTER   "       "         "

2/Lieut K de L JACOB   to 1/5 D.C.L.I. Regt 1/3/19
2/Lieut J.H. BLACKER    "          "          "
```

Captain F.G. ROGERS struck off strength 4/3/19 whilst at course U.K.
Lt W.A. BELSEY W.A. U.S.A.M.C (M.C.) struck off strength 1/3/19
2/Lieut E.T.B. SHEPHERD to 299 P.O.W. Coy off strength 3/3/19
2/Lieut G.H. HALL to U.K. Sick Struck off Strength 21/3/19
2/Lieut L ELLWOOD to 89 P.C.W. Coy off Strength 31/3/19
2/Lieut G.F.J.P. STONE) to report to Depot Exeter
2/Lieut J.A. BENJAMIN) off Strength 30/3/19

Captn Revd E FISHER (Chaplain) to 19 C.C.S

[signature] Lieut Col.
Commanding 9th (S) Battalion The Devonshire Regiment

9th (S) Battalion The Devonshire Regt

WAR DIARY

for

Month Ending 30th APRIL 1919

Army Form C. 2118.

WAR DIARY
or
INTELLIGENCE SUMMARY.
(Erase heading not required.)

April 1919

Place	Date	Hour	Summary of Events and Information	Remarks and references to Appendices
Cambrai			Owing to Battalion being reduced to cadre strength there are no men available for parades. The Bands were allotted Battalion on 8th, 17th & 29th.	
Cambrai	12th		The following Officers were appointed as shown: Capt. H.C. WILSON to be acting Captain (additional from 23/11/18) (additional from 1/12/18) 2/Lt. W.E. MANLEY MC " " " " " "	
Cambrai	14th		The following Officers proceed to POW. Coys. Capt. F. HOARE to 209 POW. Coy. 2/Lt. J.H. BRAUND " 208 " " " 2/Lt. R.J. TURNER " 208 " " " 2/Lt. F.J. PEARCE " 208 " " "	
Cambrai	15th		The following Officers proceed to POW Coys. 2/Lt. S.N. BLISS to 208 POW Coy 2/Lt. H.F. TAYLOR " " " " 2/Lt. A.G. SMITH MM " " " "	Contd.

Army Form C. 2118.

WAR DIARY
or
INTELLIGENCE SUMMARY.
(Erase heading not required.)

April 1919

Place	Date	Hour	Summary of Events and Information	Remarks and references to Appendices
Cambrai	18th		Good Friday. There were Divine Services in the English Church.	
Cambrai	19th		A Board of Officers assembled at Divisional Canteen 21 Boulevard Faidherbe to take stock. Major J.N. BRUNEAU was President.	
			There was a Kit inspection in Billets.	
Cambrai	21st		Divine Services were held (Voluntary) for the following Religions C of E, Presbyterian, Wesleyans etc., & Roman Catholic.	
Cambrai	22nd		The Divisional Cadre Sports were proposed & were held for 29th April, in Jardin Public Cambrai.	
Cambrai	27th		Divine Services were held for all Religions.	

Army Form C. 2118.

WAR DIARY
or
INTELLIGENCE SUMMARY.
(Erase heading not required.)

April 1919.

Instructions regarding War Diaries and Intelligence Summaries are contained in F. S. Regs., Part II. and the Staff Manual respectively. Title pages will be prepared in manuscript.

Place	Date	Hour	Summary of Events and Information	Remarks and references to Appendices
Cambrai	29		The Divisional Packs of sports were postponed owing to bad weather.	
Cambrai	30		Orders were received to despatch Draft of 29 N.C.O.s & men to 1/5 D.C.L. Regt.	
			Officers demobilized during month. 9.	
			Other Ranks demobilized " 11.	
			2 " Other Ranks volunteer to Police during month 1.	
			Strength of Battalion at end of month. Officers 85 Other Ranks.	
			Ration Strength 3 64 " " "	

Coote.

Army Form C. 2118.

WAR DIARY
or
INTELLIGENCE SUMMARY.
(Erase heading not required.)

April 1919

Place	Date	Hour	Summary of Events and Information	Remarks and references to Appendices
			The following Officers served with Battalion during month.	

Commanding Officer   Lt Col H I STONEY DSO
2nd in Command   Maj DW BRUNICARDI MC
Adjutant   Capt NE MANLEY MC

Capt.   R P PRIDHAM MC (and demobilized) 2/Lt R COX MC
Capt.   RPC HARVEY   "   2/Lt F J PEARCE (to POW Coy)
Capt.   J W PALMER   "   Lt   J C HITCHENS (and demobilized)
Capt.   A B T PRYNNE   Leave UK   2/Lt J D BARRIBALL (attached GOO HAVRE)
Capt.   H C WILSON (and demobilized)
Lieut. F P BONNIWELL (and demobilized)
Lieut. J F K HUGHES   — UK —
2/Lt.   G S R FARMER
2/Lt.   H M I TAYLOR   (to POW Coy)
2/Lt.   R J TURNER   ("   "   )
2/Lt.   S N BLISS   ("   "   )
2/Lt.   F   HOARE   ("   "   )
2/Lt.   J H BRAUND   ("   "   )
2/Lt.   A J E D E   (and demobilized)
Lt.   H G SMITH MM   (to POW Coy)

W Manley Capt
for Lt Col
Comdg 9th Demobiline Bn.

SECRET

9th (S) Battalion The Devonshire Regt

WAR DIARY.

for

MAY
1919

Army Form C. 2118.

WAR DIARY
or
INTELLIGENCE SUMMARY.
(Erase heading not required.)

May 1919

Instructions regarding War Diaries and Intelligence Summaries are contained in F. S. Regs., Part II. and the Staff Manual respectively. Title pages will be prepared in manuscript.

Place	Date	Hour	Summary of Events and Information	Remarks and references to Appendices
Cambrai	1st		The Battalion being at Cadre Strength there are no men available for Parades. A Draft of 29 other Ranks for 1/5 DCLI Regiment, 61st Division entrained at CAMBRAI ANNEXE, there men being struck off strength of Battalion.	
Cambrai	4th		There were Church services for all religions	
Cambrai	7th		Lt Col H. I. STOREY was admitted to hospital 7/5/19 & Captain A J F PRYNNE assumed command of Battalion from this date.	
Cambrai	8th		The Kermesse Packet Sports took place in the Jardin Publie CAMBRAI. The French Band & 25th Divisional Packet Band were in attendance. Prizes were distributed on the field.	

Army Form C. 2118.

WAR DIARY
or
INTELLIGENCE SUMMARY.
(Erase heading not required.)

May 1919

Instructions regarding War Diaries and Intelligence Summaries are contained in F. S. Regs., Part II. and the Staff Manual respectively. Title pages will be prepared in manuscript.

Place	Date	Hour	Summary of Events and Information	Remarks and references to Appendices
Cambrai	10th		The XIII Corps Group Pocket Sports were held at CAUDRY. Lorries conveyed troops from Cambrai.	
Cambrai	11th		There were Church Services for all religions.	
Cambrai	18th		Church Services.	
Cambrai	24th		The Baths were allotted to Battalion.	
Cambrai	25th		Church Services	

WAR DIARY
or
INTELLIGENCE SUMMARY
(Erase heading not required.)

Army Form C. 2118.

May 1919

Place	Date	Hour	Summary of Events and Information	Remarks and references to Appendices
Contrai			Officers Demobilized during month - One	
			Other Ranks Demobilized during month 10.	
			Hostilities admissions during Month: 1 Officer	
			1 Other Rank	
			Lt. Col. H.I. STOREY DSO	
			was admitted 7/5/19.	
			Total Strength of Battalion 31/5/19.	Officers actor par (Wastings) 52.
				1.
			Ration Strength.	Officers Other Ranks 35.
				4.
			Officers on strength of Battalion during month.	
			Commanding Officer Lt. Col. H.I. STOREY DSO	
			Capt. A.J.F. PRYNNE	2/Lt. J.F.L. HUGHES (Demobilized)
			Adjutant Capt. N/S MANLEY MC	2/Lt. E.S.R. FARMER
			Capt. MC WILSON	2/Lt. R. COX MC
			O/C Quartermaster Lt. G.W. MAYNARD	2/Lt. J.D. BARRIBALL

A.J.F. Prynne Captain.
Cmdg 9th (S) Bn The Devonshire Regt.

WAR DIARY
or
INTELLIGENCE SUMMARY.
(Erase heading not required.)

Army Form C. 2118.

9 Divs

June 1919.

45.D.

Place	Date	Hour	Summary of Events and Information	Remarks and references to Appendices
Cambrai France.	1st		Church Services for all religions.	
	6th		Captain W.E. MANLEY M.C. proceeded to join 211 POW Coy Captain A.J.F. TRYNNE " " " 234 " " Captain H.C. WILSON " " " 234 " " and were struck off strength of Battalion	
	14th		The Cadre, consisting of 1 Officer 2 Warrant Officers & 22 other Ranks proceeded to Demobilization Camp Cambrai for dispersal to U.K. 1 Officer & 12 Other Ranks were left behind to form Equipment Guard over stores etc.	
	15th		The Cadre entrained at CAMBRAI VILLE station at 7 hrs on Sunday morning 15th June 1919.	

Contd.

Army Form C. 2118.

WAR DIARY
or
INTELLIGENCE SUMMARY.
(Erase heading not required.)

Instructions regarding War Diaries and Intelligence Summaries are contained in F. S. Regs., Part II. and the Staff Manual respectively. Title pages will be prepared in manuscript.

Place	Date	Hour	Summary of Events and Information	Remarks and references to Appendices
	18		The Cadre landed at Dover at 11.30 hrs and entrained for Victoria Station London. At 22.00 hrs they left Paddington for Exeter.	
	19		The Cadre arrived at Exeter in the early hours (2 am) and marched to the depot where the O.C. Depot was roused, the Colours handed over & the men put under canvas, owing to the arrival had been dispatched but unfortunately was not opened, and there was no reception.	
Cambrai	24		To celebrate the acceptance of Peace Treaty there was a procession of French & English soldiers & civilians, commencing at 9 am & finishing about 10.30 am. The French Band leading the procession.	

Army Form C. 2118.

WAR DIARY
or
INTELLIGENCE SUMMARY.
(Erase heading not required.)

Instructions regarding War Diaries and Intelligence Summaries are contained in F. S. Regs., Part II. and the Staff Manual respectively. Title pages will be prepared in manuscript.

Place	Date	Hour	Summary of Events and Information	Remarks and references to Appendices
Cambrai	26th		To celebrate Goose there were entertainments & sports held at Cambrai. Cain arranged trips from Cambrai.	
Cambrai	27th		There were also Aquatic sports at the Swimming Baths Petit Cambrai on Tuesday June 27th commencing at 2.30 p.m.	
Cambrai	28th			
Cambrai	29th			

WAR DIARY
or
INTELLIGENCE SUMMARY.
(Erase heading not required.)

Army Form C. 2118.

Officers demobilised during month Nil
Other Ranks " " Under 24.

Entire strength of Battalion 4 Officers 12 Other Ranks.

Officers on strength of Battalion during Month

Lt-Col H I STOREY DSO. (Argyle)
Captain A J C PRYNNE (to 234 POW Bn)
Captain H C WILSON (to 234 POW Bn)
Captain W E MANNEY MC (to 234 POW Bn)
2/Lt R COX MC
Lt F W MAYNARD
Lt J D BARRIS RAN (attached COO Stores)

Army Equipment Issues of Devon Regt.

Nor Spr.

www.ingramcontent.com/pod-product-compliance
Lightning Source LLC
Chambersburg PA
CBHW081240170426
43191CB00034B/1993